The Symbolism of Asia

An Illustrated, Introductory Guide

2nd Edition

Matthew Stavros

Vicus Lusorum

The Symbolism of Asia: An Illustrated, Introductory Guide
Second Edition
Copyright © 2020 by Matthew Stavros

Cover: The pagoda of Ulun Danu Batur Temple in the district of Kintamani, Bali, Indonesia. Author's work.

ISBN: 9798636464549

Also available on Kindle via www.amazon.com

For Kent

About the Author

Matthew Stavros is a historian of Japan and the author of *Kyoto: An Urban History of Japan's Premodern Capital* (University of Hawai'i Press, 2014) and over a dozen articles on Kyoto's architectural and urban history. His research focuses primarily on the material culture of premodern Japan and eastern Asia, with special interest in cities, buildings, and monuments. He trained in architectural and urban history at Kyoto University and read history at Princeton University where he earned a PhD. He has taught on all periods of Japanese history and historiography, research methods in Asian Studies, Sino-Japanese diplomatics, and more broadly on the histories and cultures of East and Southeast Asia. He is the director of the Kyoto Consortium for Japanese Studies.

www.mstavros.com | www.kyotohistory.com

Table of Contents

About the Author

Section 1
Symbolism

The world is filled with symbols. They permeate our civilizations and define our cultures. They can be as simple as a wooden cross or the silhouette of an intersecting hammer and sickle.

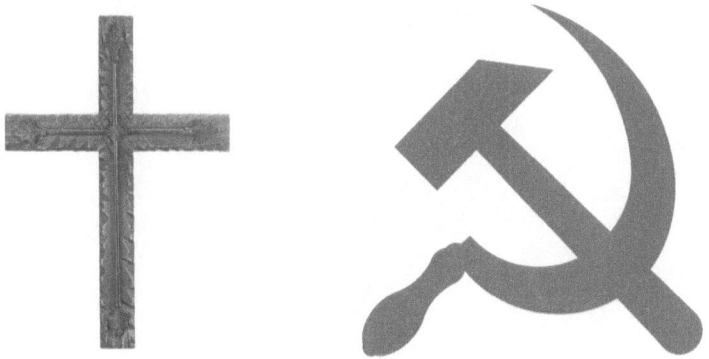

Symbols are abbreviated signifiers, catalysts that remind viewers of deeper stories, legends, or shared experiences. Easily hoisted above a crowd or emblazoned onto a throne, they can be used to rally forces or instill a sense of belonging. They tie people together into imagined communities, justifying inspiring acts of heroism just as often as unimaginable atrocities.

But symbols have no value if people do not understand them. We need to know the stories and myths behind them in order to appreciate their meanings. If we do not, they are lifeless objects with no deeper significance. Not only will they fail to inspire, it is entirely possible we will not even notice that they are there.

This book aims to help readers recognize the hallmark symbols of Asian civilizations and to read them for their cultural, social and religious significance. Acquiring this skill provides a level of cultural literacy that heightens awareness to the social, religious and political currents that surround and penetrate so many Asian contexts. Many of the symbols examined in this book cut across countries, giving the whole region a striking degree of homogeneity that transcends languages, national boundaries, and ethnicities.

In order to read symbols for their historical and cultural meanings, it is first necessary to know what to look for. One must know the backstories and possible interpretations. But, by their very nature, symbols are open to a wide variety of interpretations. Anyone who claims that a particular symbol always and everywhere has one particular meaning is probably not aware of other interpretations. Either that or they have a biased agenda. The truth is that symbols not only have different meanings to different peoples in different places, over time their meanings often change.

This book is not exhaustive. It focuses on a small but powerful set of images and shapes that appear frequently in the art, architecture, and monuments of Asia. What is included in this slim volume is only the tip of the iceberg. There are many conflicting views and theories, which can be frustrating. At the same time, it can serve as a good reminder that there remains a lot of research to be done.

Chapter 1
The Swastika

The swastika is one of the most divisive and vilified symbols of the modern era. Used by the Nazis until 1945 as the emblem of their party and cause, in many parts of the world, the symbol is closely associated with racism, bigotry, and authoritarianism.

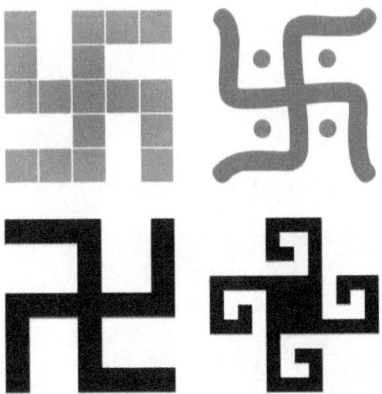

Forget everything you know about the swastika

The original symbol, which is ancient, had nothing to do with the Nazis. In fact, in the grand arc of human history, this twisted little cross has most often had an overwhelmingly positive nuance and it is still used throughout Asia to represent things that are good, sacred, and auspicious. To this day, the swastika is a sacred symbol in Hinduism, Buddhism, Jainism, and Odinism. It can be found adorning temples, shrines, and houses across Asia.

In fact, right up until the Nazi transformed the swastikas into a symbol of evil in the 1930s, it was used widely across Europe and America to sell products from fruit to Coca-Cola.[1]

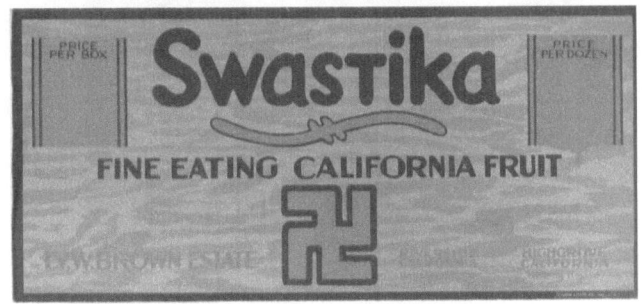

The world's first symbol?

The swastika goes back so far in human civilization that some scholars claim it is among the world's oldest symbols. Archaeologists have found samples across Eurasia that are over 5,000 years old. Here are a few examples:

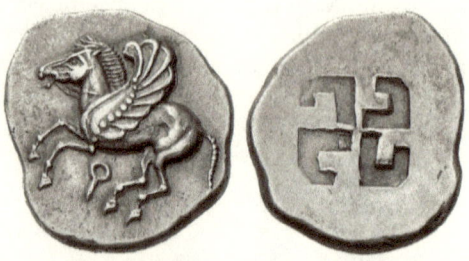

Swastika on a Greek silver stater coin from Corinth, 6th c BCE.[2]

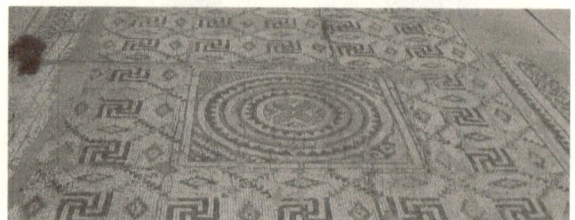

Mosaic swastika in excavated Byzantine church in Shavei Tzion (Israel).[3]

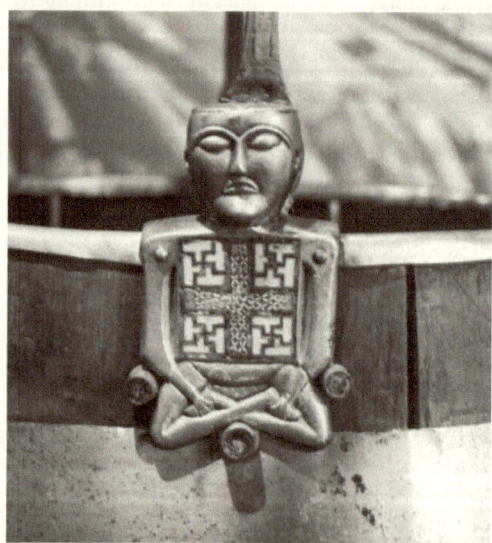

Four swastikas on a bucket found on the Viking Oseberg ship (ca. CE 800).[4]

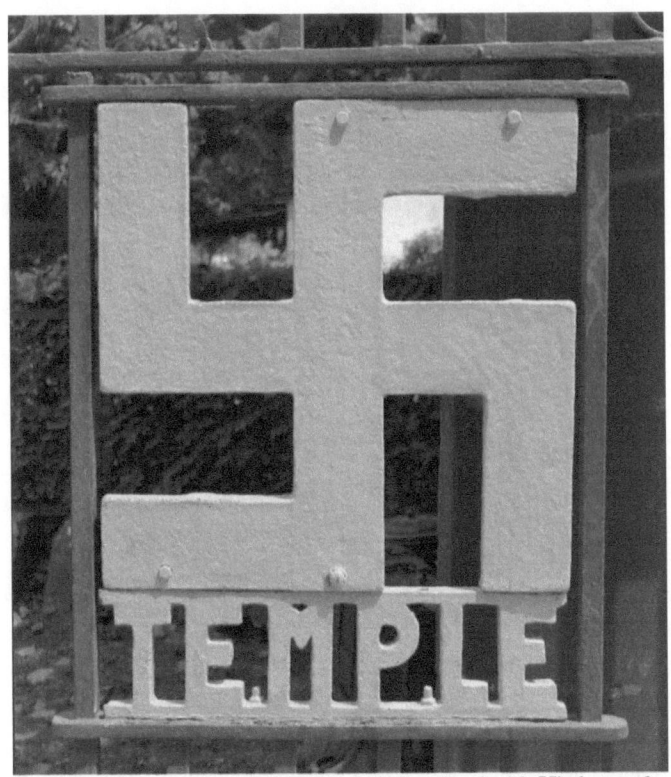

Swastika are ubiquitous in India, frequently associated with Hindu temples.[5]

Swastika are common in Japan and other East Asian countries today.

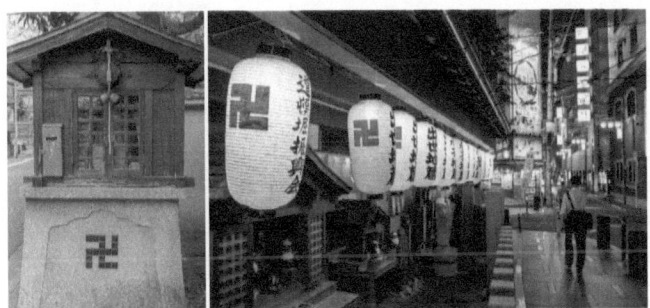

Corner shrines in Japan. Author's work.

Aniconic vs Iconic

Many readers will be familiar with the word "iconic," meaning to "look like something." A Christian icon, for example, could be a small crucifix or the painting of a saint. Both items look like the thing they represent. A national icon might be the silhouette of a national hero or animal. An "icon" is a literal depiction of an actual thing in a non-abstract way.

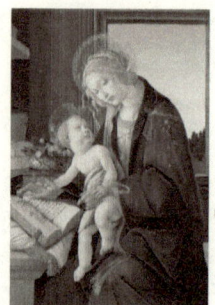 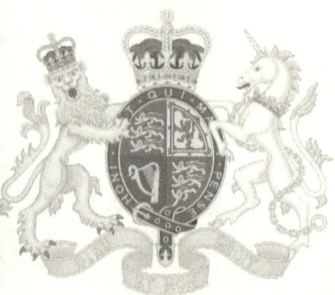

Classic examples of "icons." Mary and Jesus (left) and the Coat of Arms of the United Kingdom (right), which includes icons of the British and Scottish national animals (lion and unicorn).

"Aniconic" is just the opposite. It is abstract. It is symbolic or suggestive rather than literal. It represents something, but just by looking at it, one would never know what. A viewer must know the stories, myths and ideas within which the image was formulated and used. The swastika is a quintessential example of an aniconic symbol. By itself, it means nothing. In context it means a lot.

Long before followers began depicting the Buddha as a person, he was represented using aniconic symbols. The most common were footprints, lotus flowers, umbrellas and the Bodhi tree. This image of a stone carving in the collection of Yale University includes several of these symbols as well as swastikas on the toe prints.

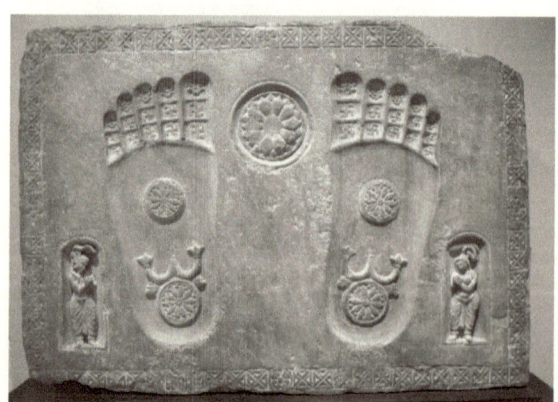

Footprints of the Buddha (Buddhapada). 2nd c. CE. [6]

Aniconic symbols were common in the ancient world. Explanations for why are various and open to debate, but several are quite convincing. First, aniconic symbols are easy to make. Compare, for example, the drawing of a swastika with the carving of a stone statue in human form. The latter is much more difficult and can only be done by very skilled people at great cost. Second, in some societies and religions (just like in Islam today) representing a God or sacred being is forbidden. If you cannot draw a picture of God, creating a symbol to represent her is the next best thing.

The Meaning of the Swastika (long before the Nazis)

It appears the swastika may have originated among Indo-Aryan peoples who, many thousands of years ago, spread their culture and language from central Asia into India and across Europe.

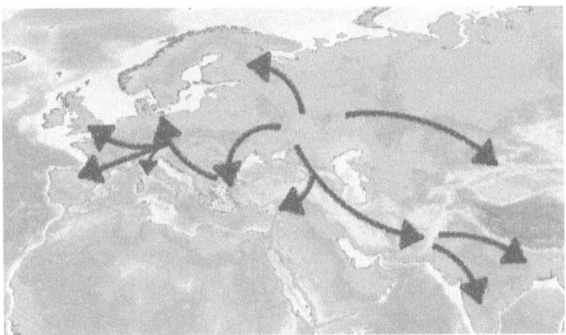

Indo-Aryan Migration map.

The word swastika comes from the Sanskrit term *svastika*, which means "good fortune" or "well-being." The same root word informs the Thai salutation *sawatdee*, which has a similar meaning.

In ancient Norse, Viking and other northern European traditions, the swastika is thought to have represented thunder or lightning and is tied to reverence for the mythical god Thor. This association with lightning is interesting because, as we shall see below, lightning symbolism permeates many Asian cultures too.

According to René Guénon, the swastika represents rotational movement around a center or immutable axis (Latin: axis mundi, "axis of the world"). As such, it is a symbol of cosmic order and the existence of an absolute God or ruler who rules in harmony with the cosmos.[7] This notion of a cosmic center or "world axis" is also a theme that recurs often in the study of Asian symbolism. Axes mundi appear frequently in Buddhist and Hindu stories, cosmologies, and art.

In Hinduism, the clockwise swastika is said to symbolize *surya* (the sun), prosperity and good luck. The counterclockwise symbol, which is called *sauvastika*, symbolizes night, passivity or the feminine. This dichotomy between light and dark is common in Asian symbolism and will reappear several times in below.

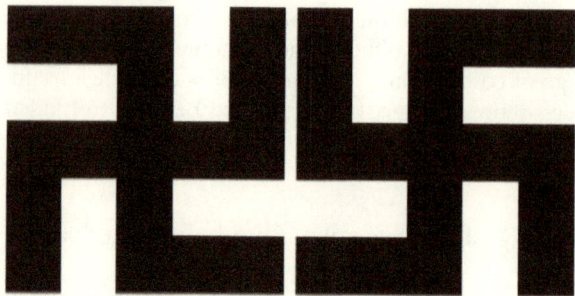

The swastika can "spin" in either direction and is thought to have different meanings depending on its direction. Author's work.

The Nazi Adoption of the Swastika

There was a lot of interest in ancient civilizations during the 19th century. When research emerged about Aryan civilization, which was thought to be a common progenitor of Indo-European people, the Nazis seized on the idea and applied it to their own notion of a "master race" and "racial purity." [8] Using a twisted logic and an incorrect understanding of history, for them, the swastika was a symbol of their own "Aryan identity" and, by relation, German nationalist pride. The Nazi Party formally adopted the swastika as its symbol in 1920.[9] Today, the symbol is banned in the Federal Republic of Germany.

Chapter 2
Yin-Yang

In Chinese philosophy, yin and yang describe how seemingly opposite forces may actually be complementary, interconnected, and symbiotic in the natural world. This concept traces its origins to the roots of Chinese civilization (at least 2000 BCE) and has inspired people across Asia. It is the core tenet of Taoism, a philosophy that focuses on the harmony of cosmic forces that flow through all things.

Although yin-yang has no single standard representation, it is most often associated with the *taijitu* (simplified Chinese: 太极图; traditional Chinese: 太極圖), a circle composed of sharply contrasting colors that "swirl" around a shared center. The *taijitu* is the centerpiece of the South Korean flag and has been popularized by artists around the world who use it as a generic symbol to signify Asia or something Asian.

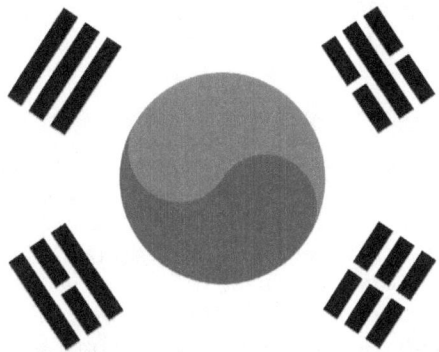

The flag of South Korea, a taijitu "swirl" surrounded by divination symbols.

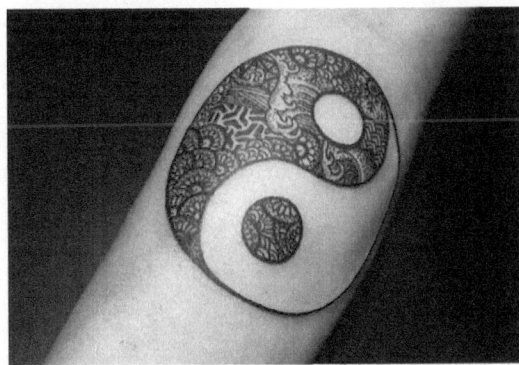

The yin-yang "swirl" (taijitu) is often used in tattoos.

The Meaning of Yin-Yang

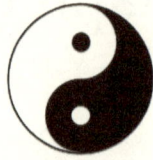

The yin-yang symbol represents opposites in balance, a harmonic association of dark and light, passive and active, female and male, shade and sun. Yin is the dark side and yang is the light side.

Yin is characterized as slow, soft, yielding, diffuse, cold, wet, and passive; and is associated with water, earth, the moon, femininity, and night time.

Yang is fast, hard, solid, focused, hot, dry, and active; and is associated with fire, sky, the sun, masculinity and daytime.

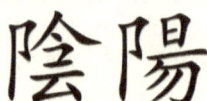

Yin (left) and yang (right) as written in traditional Chinese characters. In Japanese, they are read "in-yō."

Influence

The ideas that underpin yin-yang have inspired a broad spectrum of human endeavors, including philosophy, politics, art, architecture and urban planning. They are central to historical Chinese philosophy and statecraft. Chinese emperors—the vast majority of whom were Taoist—gained their legitimacy by claiming to have earned the Mandate of Heaven. The Mandate could be withdrawn, however, if the ruler did not operate in harmony with the forces of nature. Force and coercion must be balanced by benevolence and advocacy; war with peace, and rewards with punishments. The same ideas informed the political philosophy of Korea's long Joseon dynasty (1392-1897). It is for this reason that the yin-yang symbol appears in that country's modern flag.

In Japan, not many emperors attempted to actually rule. Emperor Kanmu (736-806 CE), however, was an exception and his portrait suggests he drew heavily on continental symbolism to assert legitimacy. The sun and moon drawn over his head, for example, likely reflect ying and yang thought.

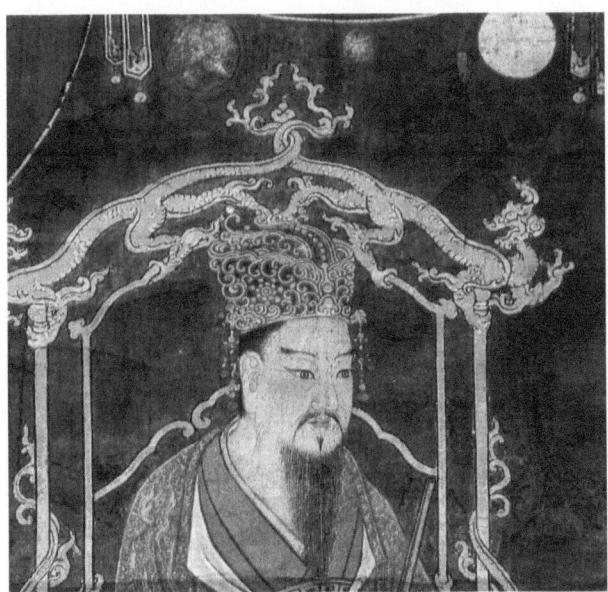
Emperor Kanmu's portrait, section.

In architecture, yin-yang shaped the way buildings were planned and oriented. We see this in Japan, for example, where historical texts frequently refer to palaces having two distinct sides. One was "sunny," "bright," "clean," and "official" (晴) while the other was "shaded," "dirty," and "mundane" (穢). The former was reserved for public rituals, events, and official business while the latter was private space, used for eating, sleeping, bathing, and informal activities. Incidentally, directional theories across Asia were northern-centric: the south was the direction of good lighting, warmth, and officialdom. Had these ideas emerged in the southern hemisphere, auspicious directions would have likely been reversed.

Comparable ideas Beyond East Asia

In mainstream Indian philosophies, creation and destruction are considered to be fundamentally interrelated. They exist on a fluid continuum; they are like two sides of the same coin. Creation cannot exist without destruction and vice versa. We see this principle reflected in the sacred dance of Shiva Nataraja, who is both the creator and the destroyer of worlds. According to James Lochtefeld, Shiva's dance encompasses creation, destruction and all things in between.[10]

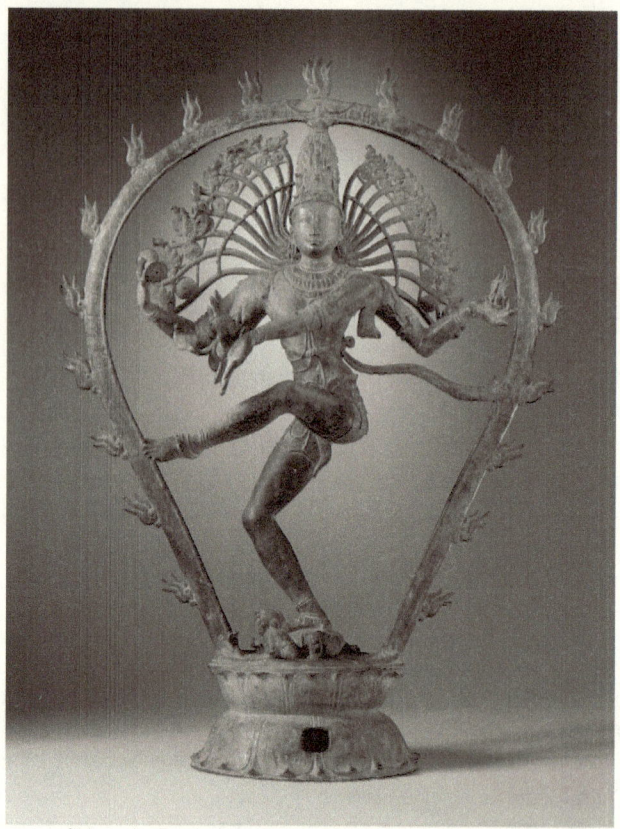

Shiva, the Lord of the Dance (Shiva Nataraja), 10th c.[11]

The basic idea behind yin-yang might also be compared to Jewish and Christian ideas of God being the Alpha and the Omega, the "beginning and the end." Such a parallel suggests there was widespread belief that opposite ends of a spectrum are co-dependent and complimentary.

Interested readers should look into Taoism and the *I Ching* for more information.

Chapter 3
Lingam and Yoni

The lingam and yoni are similar to yin and yang in the way they represent two opposite-yet-complementary forces. In the case of lingam and yoni, the focus is on the union of male and female energies. The lingam represents the male and the yoni represents the female. They frequently appear together.

Although lingam and yoni are often associated with veneration of the Indian creator god Shiva and his counterpart Shakti, the ideas that underpin the symbolism are practically universal. Procreation is, after all, the essential biological force. It sustains species, families, and civilizations. It also transforms parents into creators of life, something that can be considered a god-like ability. It is for these reasons that fertility cults are so common in human history and why having children is considered a sacred act, even a duty, by many religions.

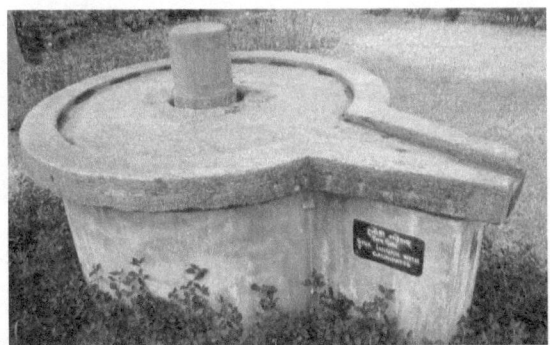

Shiva Lingam with Gauripatta, Mahasthangarh Museum, Bogra, Bangladesh.[12]

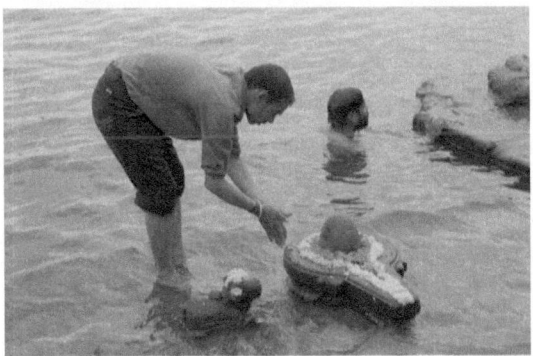

Saivism ritual, flower decoration of Linga, Madhya Pradesh India.[13]

Lingam and yoni are aniconic symbols most frequently found in India and Southeast Asia. They have vaguely anatomical shapes, but tend not to be as phallic as, for example, the foci of penis cults found in some countries.

In its stylized form, the lingam is thought to represent a cosmic pillar or axis. It emanates its all-producing energy to the four quarters of the universe. Yoni, the female counterpart, often forms the base from which the lingam rises. The word "yoni" is sometimes translated as "womb." Although the lingam originally may have had no relation to Shiva, it has, from ancient times, been regarded as symbolizing Shiva's creative energy and is widely worshipped as his fundamental form.

Indian religious art has never shied away from the topic of sex or what may be called "eroticism." This is due to the tantric tradition. Tantra takes the approach that one should not reject the body and its desires, but instead embrace them on the road to enlightenment. Yoga is central to this idea and it is the most widely practiced form of tantra. The tradition, however, extends to encompass the view that sexual intercourse can be sacred and a means of attaining enlightenment.

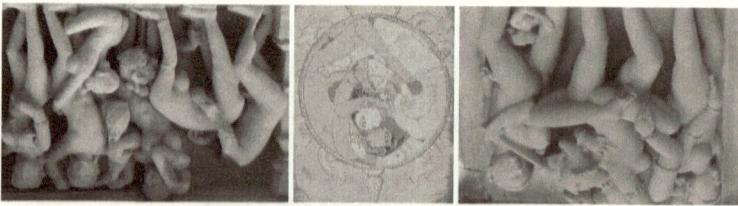

Examples of sexual tantric art in India.

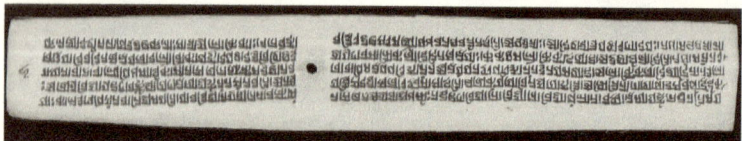

Many readers will have heard of the Kama Sutra (pictured here), an ancient Sanskrit text on sexuality, eroticism and emotional fulfillment.[14] It was written between the 1st and 6th centuries CE. The Kama Sutra is neither exclusively nor predominantly a sex manual. Rather, it is written as a guide to the "art of living," the nature of love, finding a life partner, maintaining one's love life, and other aspects pertaining to pleasure-oriented faculties of human life.

Chapter 4
Lions

Lions are the king of animals. They are proud, majestic, and have no natural predators. Throughout much of history, the lion has been considered a symbol of royalty and protection, as well as of wisdom and pride. The iconographic representation of the lion is thought to have originated in Persia at least 1000 years before the common era and spread to India and then to East Asia. Lion statues are now ubiquitous across Asia, found most frequently at the gates to shrines, temples and palaces.

The Lion in India

In India, lions came to represent the Buddha from about the time of Ashoka the Great (304-232 BCE). After unifying the expansive Mauryan Dynasty, Ashoka promoted the spread of Buddhist-like teachings through the creation of massive stone pillars. Ashokan pillars were often capped by three lions facing outward, simultaneously representing the Buddha, Ashoka himself, and the power of the state.

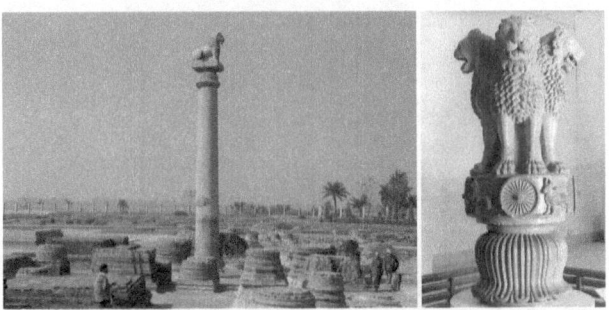

A classic example of an Ashokan Pillar (left) and the lion capital from the earliest known pillar at Sarnath, India (250 BCE).[15]

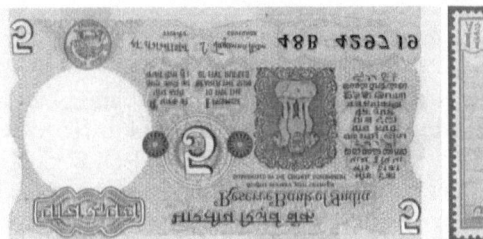

When India gained independence in 1947, the lion was adopted as a national symbol due to its historic association with unification under Ashoka. Modern Indian rupee (left) and Indian stamp from 1947.

In East and Southeast Asia

Lion symbolism arrived in China along with the earliest transmission of Buddhism from India during the Han dynasty (206 BCE-CE 220). Statues of guardian lions have traditionally stood on the sides of entrances to imperial palaces and tombs, government offices, temples, and the homes of government officials and the wealthy. They were believed to have powerful mythic protective benefits.

Across East and Southeast Asia, lions usually appear in pairs, one being male and the other, female. In China, the male usually rests his paw on an ornately embroidered ball while the female protects a cub. This gender opposition has inspired some scholars to conclude the lion pairing is related to yin and yang thought, which holds that opposing forces are often complimentary, providing for balance and harmony. In this respect, it makes sense for a leader to place lions outside his or her palace to suggest that they themselves are living and working in harmony with the universe.

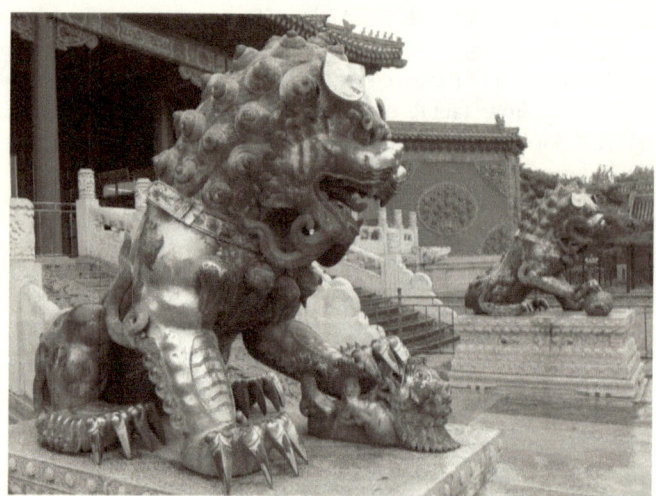

Guardian lions outside the Forbidden City, Beijing, China. The female with her supine cub is in the foreground.[16]

In many parts of Asia, the male lion is represented with his mouth open while the female's mouth is closed. In Japan, it is widely believed that the shape of the lions' mouths represents the intoning of the first and last letters of the Sanskrit alphabet, Ah and Om. Together, they symbolically represent the beginning and the end of all things. Here again, we see parallels with yin-yang and the employment of an alphabet to suggest beginning and end, birth and death, and all possible outcomes (from Alpha to Omega).[17]

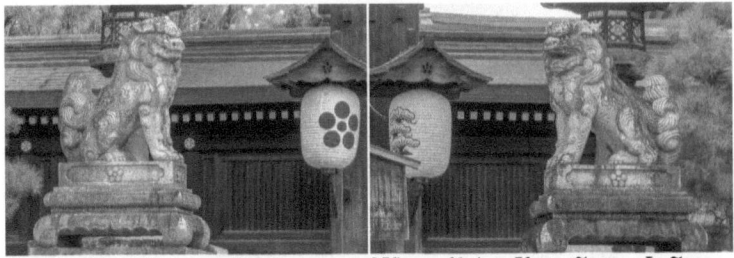

A pair of stone lions guard the entrance of Kitano Shrine, Kyoto, Japan. In Japan, they are most often called komainu 狛犬, meaning "Korean dog." The male on the right is intoning "Ah" and the female on the left is intoning "Om." Author's work.

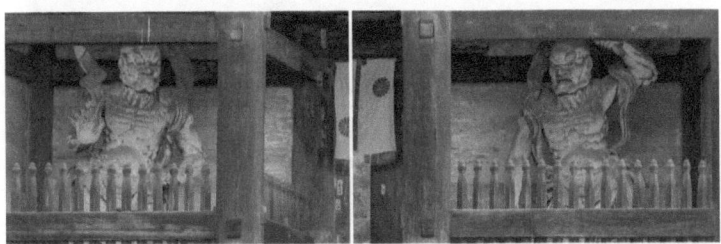

The massive and muscular Niō (仁王) statues that stand outside many Buddhist temples in East Asia also have their mouths poised in the "Ah" / "Om" shapes. The violence that characterise these imposing figures is justified by the teaching that force may sometimes be necessary in the battle against ignorance and illusion. Author's work.

Lion Icons in Europe

Lion symbolism is not limited to Asia. In fact, lions are found in the Coat of Arms of Britain and many other Anglo institutions.

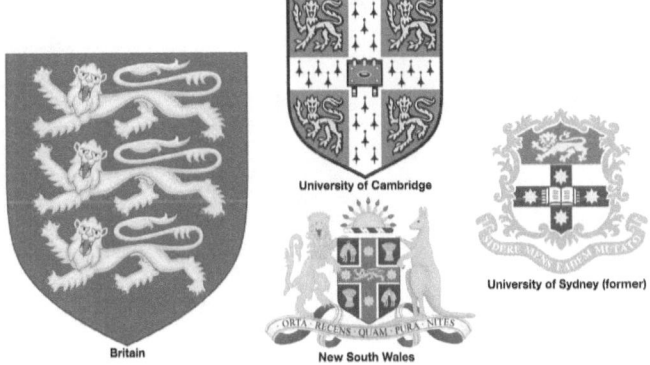

University of Cambridge

University of Sydney (former)

Britain

New South Wales

We also find lions in Germany. From 1085 to 1803, there was a state of the Holy Roman Empire in southwest Germany called the Country Palatine. The prince of Palatine, based primarily at the castle of

Heidelberg, used the lion as his symbol. To this day, the lion features prominently in and around Heidelberg.

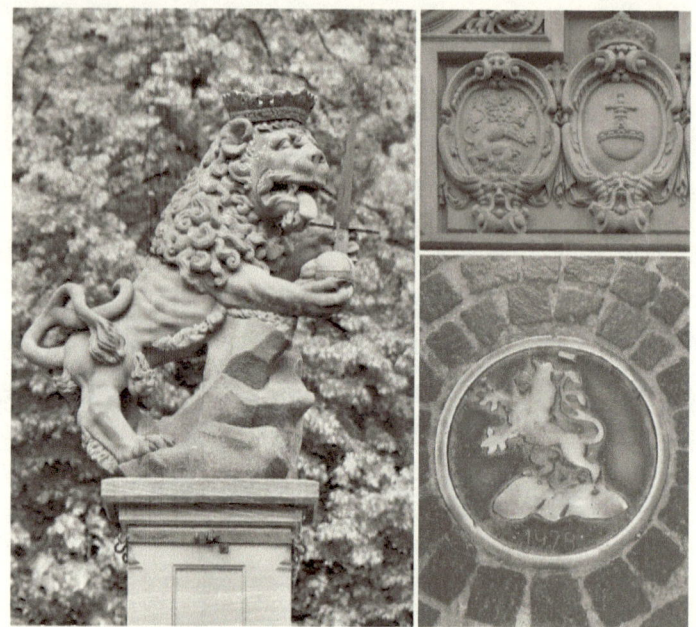

Lion emblems in and around Heidelberg, Germany. Author's work.

Chapter 5
Dragons

Dragons can be found in symbols and crests in many cultures. Although today they are most closely associated with Chinese culture, many scholars believe dragon symbolism may have originated in the Middle East (particularly Persia (modern Iran)) and India as early as the second millennium BCE.

Ancient Indian sources like the *Rig Veda* (one of the oldest texts in the world, dated around 1500 BCE) include stories of a great dragon that had to be killed by the god Indra to release the waters of heaven. In Mesopotamia, the god Marduk battled with a dragon for supremacy over human beings. In the Zoroastrian tradition of Persia, dragons were known as demonic creatures "who swallowed horses, who swallowed men... over whom poison flowed the height of a spear."[18]

A similar image inspired representations of dragons in Europe where they have generally been considered menacing and dangerous. Snarling, evil, and probably breathing fire, such images inspire the frightful depictions we see today in, for example, the *Game of Thrones* or *Harry Potter*.

The Dragon in China and East Asia

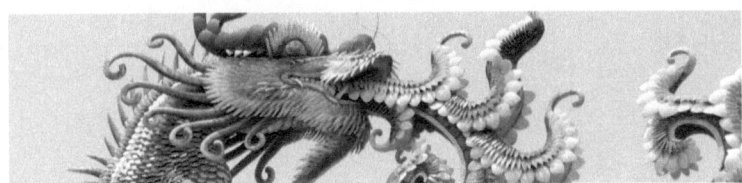

In contrast to the Middle East and Europe, the dragon took on an extremely positive image in China and those surrounding countries that adopted Chinese culture. Across East Asia, in places like Korea, Japan and Vietnam, the dragon symbolizes potent and auspicious powers, particularly control over water, rainfall, typhoons, and floods. It is a symbol of power, strength, and good luck.

China's first legendary ruler, the Yellow Emperor Huangdi, was said to have transformed into a dragon before ascending to heaven following his death. The other legendary Chinese ruler, the Yan Emperor, was born after his mother communed with a mythical dragon. Since the earliest times, Chinese rulers have employed the dragon as their symbol of power. It is for this reason that Chinese emperors were said to sit upon the "dragon throne." By association, numerous dragon images and carvings can be found in places of imperial significance throughout China. (Vietnamese rulers also occupied a "dragon throne," but Korean kings used a "phoenix throne" while Japanese emperors continue to occupy the "chrysanthemum throne").

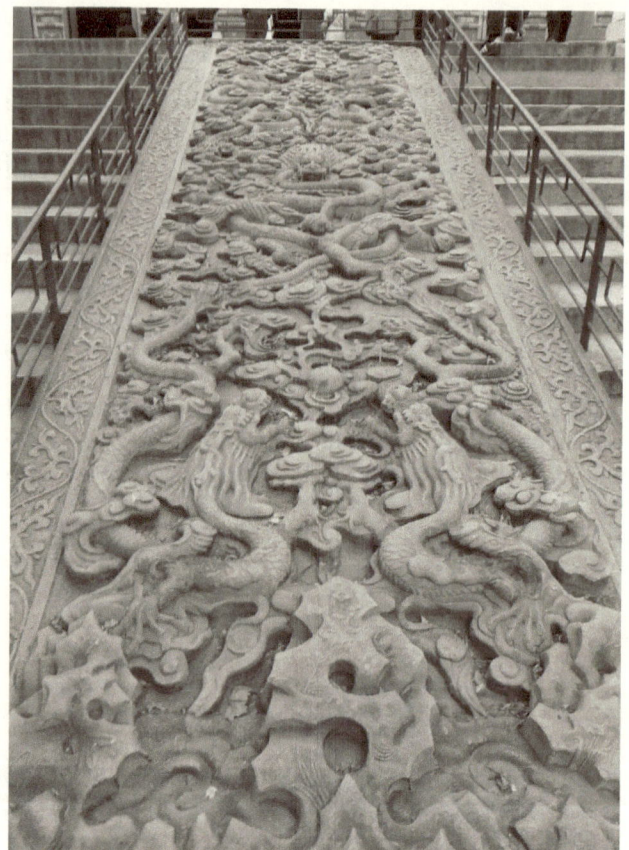

This stone dragon passage leading to the Confucius Temple in Beijing was reserved expressly for use by the reigning emperor. A similar passage can be found at the Forbidden City.[19]

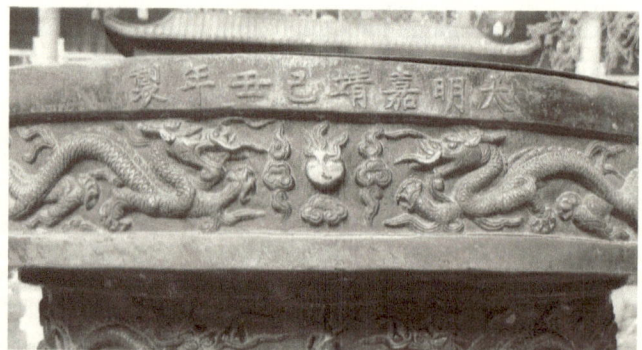

Dragons adorn a bronze incense kettle at Beijing's Temple of Heaven.[20]

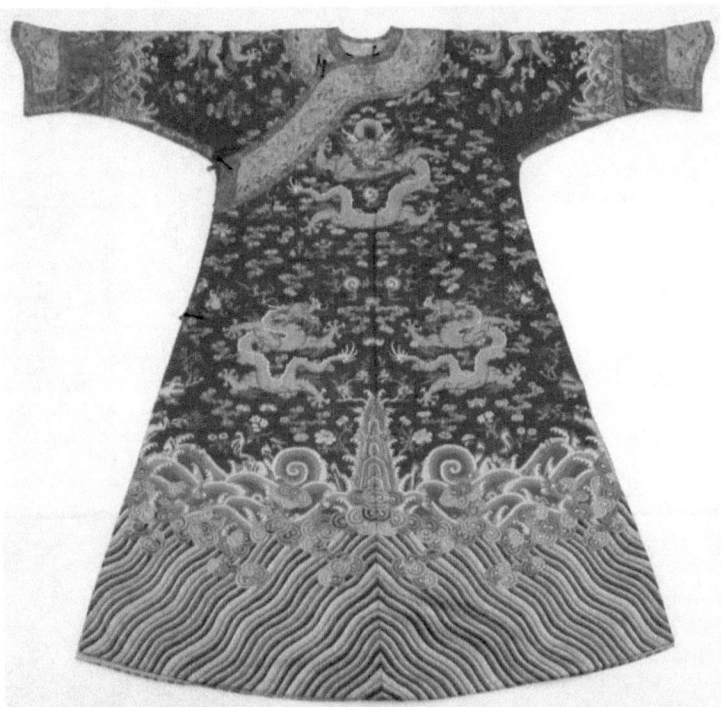

Dragons also feature prominently in the robes worn by Chinese sovereigns. This one is from the Qing dynasty (1644-1911), 18th century.[21]

Dragons arrived in Korea and Japan along with the systematic incorporation of Chinese culture starting in about the fifth or sixth centuries. During the thirteenth century, Zen Buddhism was transmitted to Japan from China, and with it came a new surge of dragon representation. In Zen philosophy, the dragon plays many roles: as a symbol of enlightenment and also as a symbol for the practitioner. For example, "meeting the dragon in the cave" is a metaphor for confronting one's deepest fears and obstacles. In Tibetan Buddhism, the thunderous voice of a dragon has the capacity of waking us from delusion.

Today, dragons adorn the roofs and gates of many temples, both as guardians and to symbolize the creature's power of clarity. Buddhist dragons are often depicted holding a jewel or a pearl. Pearls work as a useful metaphor. Despite originating from impurity (a grain of irritating sand within the oyster), the pearl becomes refined and beautiful over time, just like the spirit of a person who seeks enlightenment through dedicated practice.

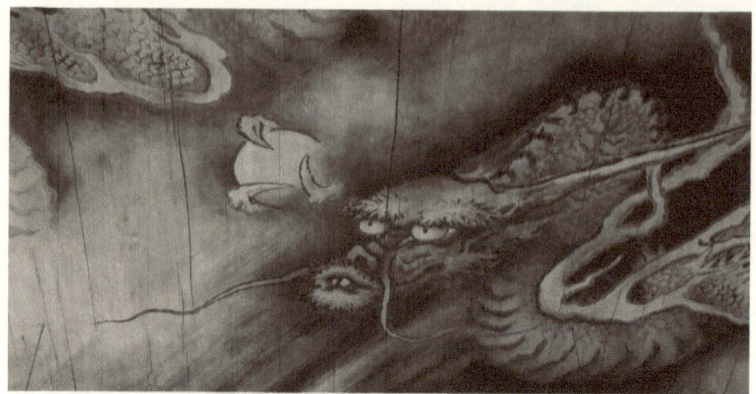

Dragons adorn many ceilings within major Zen temples. This one is from the temple of Tōfukuji in Kyoto, Kyoto. Notice the pearl, a symbol of enlightenment potential. Author's work.

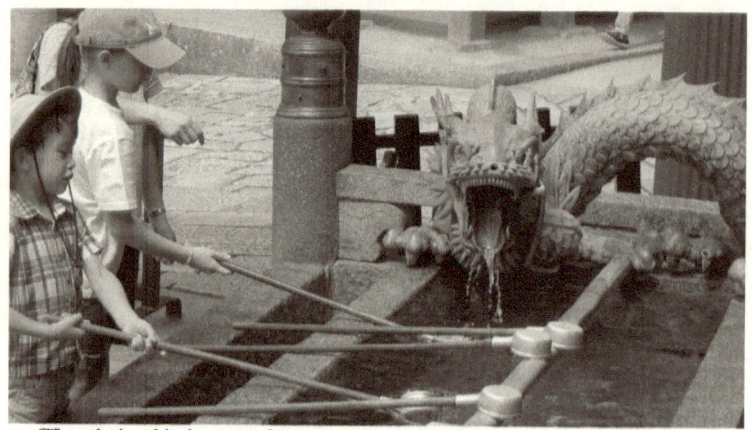

The relationship between dragons and water is clearly evident from this bronze fountain outside the temple of Kiyomizu 清水寺 in Kyoto. Author's work.

Morphology

Around the world, dragons are depicted in strikingly similar ways. The resemblance is remarkable when we consider the profound differences between the many societies where they are found. Whether it be in Persia, India or Vietnam, dragons tend to be serpentine creatures, with four legs, scales, large claws and threatening teeth.

Chinese mythology describes the dragon as a composite beast, with features resembling several animals. Citing a variety of primary sources, the Sinologist Henri Doré claims that an "authentic dragon" in Chinese culture should have the antlers of a deer, the head of a crocodile, a demon's eyes, the neck of a snake, a tortoise's abdomen, a hawk's claws, the palms of a tiger, and a cow's ears.[22]

Many representations also include wings that are disproportionately small compared to the body. The small size can be explained by noting that dragons in Chinese and East Asian cultures are often considered waterborne creatures. Although they may be found in the sky, it is most useful to think of them as "swimming" through clouds and rain rather than navigating the air like a bird.

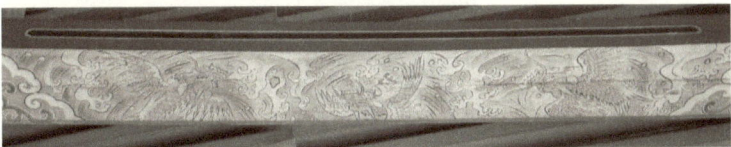

This illustration on the rafters of the temple of Rokuhara Mitsuji in Kyoto, Japan depicts dragons with features resembling fish. The water motif is obvious. Author's work.

Different dragons have different numbers of claws. During several long dynasties in Chinese history, five-clawed dragons were reserved for use by the emperor, on his clothing and palaces. Four-clawed dragons could be used as ornaments by princes and members of the nobility. Many of the dragons found at Zen temples clutch a pearl with only three claws. There's no scholarly consensus on the meanings behind the different numbers, however, circumstantial evidence suggests that it is best not to assume more is necessarily better.

Dragons have much in common with several other mythical creatures and are sometimes morphologically "blended" with them. See, for example, *nagas*, *kalas* and *makaras*.

Chapter 6
Dharmachakra: Dharma Wheels

The historical Buddha was born Siddhartha Gautama in the northern Indian subcontinent around 500 BCE. He was the prince of a warrior clan whose leaders regularly became local kings. At his birth, there was a prophecy that he would be a "Cakravārtin," which is an ambiguous Sanskrit terms that could mean either "world conquered" or a "world renouncer."

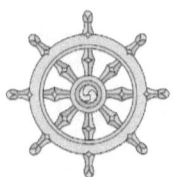

For Siddhartha to become a "world conqueror" would mean that he followed in his father's footsteps and became a warrior-king (*kshatriya*) who, through ruling, would "turn the wheel of the world." In contrast, if he were to become a "world renouncer," he would leave the world of power and wealth and instead "turn the wheel of the Dharma." He would seek enlightenment. Incidentally, Siddhartha's father wanted his son to become a king, not an ascetic. Siddhartha obviously did not listen!

Buddhist Kingship

Over time, the two ostensibly contradictory ideas of the Cakravārtin became united within a single ideology of Buddhist kingship. The ideal king, called Cakravārtin, would be *both* a world conqueror and a world renouncer. He would govern the political realm (the *artha*) in perfect harmony with the Buddhist law (the Dharma). He would unify sacred and secular authority. Out of respect for such a vaunted ideal, "Cakravārtin" is often translated as "universal monarch." Another related Sanskrit term is "*dharmaraja*," which literally means "dharma king."

Ashoka and the Dharmachakra

According to tradition, Ashoka the Great (304-232 BCE) is widely considered the first "Cakravārtin," someone who turned both the wheel of the world and the wheel of the Dharma as the ideal ruler. In the 3rd century BCE, Ashoka unified most of the Indian subcontinent through military force before seeking to rule in accordance with Buddhism or

Buddhist-like teachings. The "dharmachakra" or "dharma wheel" became Ashoka's symbol!

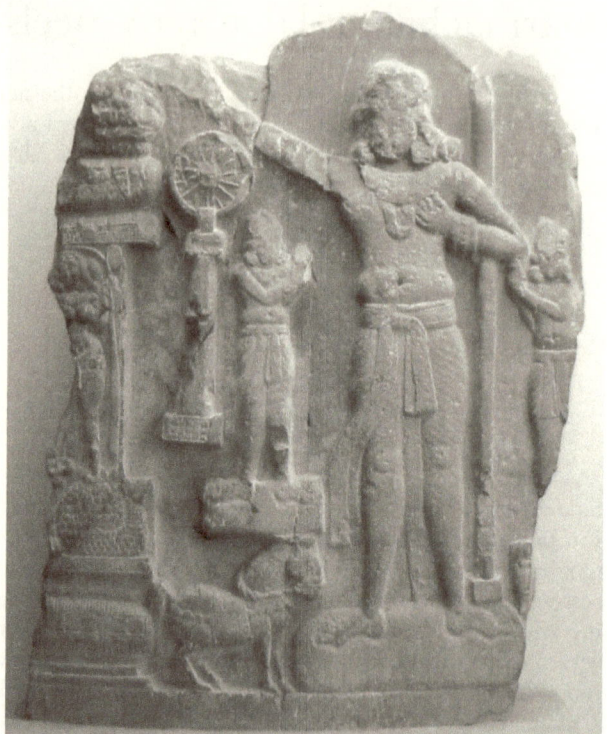

This stone carving is widely thought to depict Ashoka turning the dharmachakra. Dated roughly to about the year 1.[23]

Ashoka has long embodied Indian ideas of unity and virtuous rule. Because of the association, his dharmachakra became a symbol of the country, found today in the Indian flag and currency.

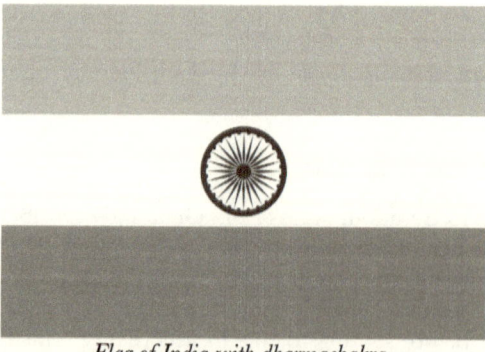

Flag of India with dharmachakra.

Dharmachakra Across Asia

As the Cakravārtin ideal spread across Asia from about the 3rd century BCE, the symbolism of the dharmachakra moved with it. Whenever it is found, the wheel represents Buddhism in the same way that a cross represents Christianity, or the Star of David represents Judaism. There are also political valances. The wheels often signify that the leaders who first adopted Buddhism sought to legitimize their rule using specifically Hindu-Buddhist idioms of kingship. It represents an attempt to sacralize one's rule. That is, to justify their leadership in terms of sacred authority, not just military power, wealthy or status.

Today, besides in India, dharmachakra are found most frequently in Tibet, Southeast Asia and Japan. Each of those places have a rich history of rulers claiming to be "universal monarchs" and/or "dharma kings." In Japan, it was usually not the reigning emperor who made such a claim. Instead, it was an ex-sovereign or a warrior-aristocrat who had retired and undergone special religious rituals before claiming the title of *hōō* 法皇, meaning "dharma king." Examples include Shirakawa, Goshirakawa, and Ashikaga Yoshimitsu.

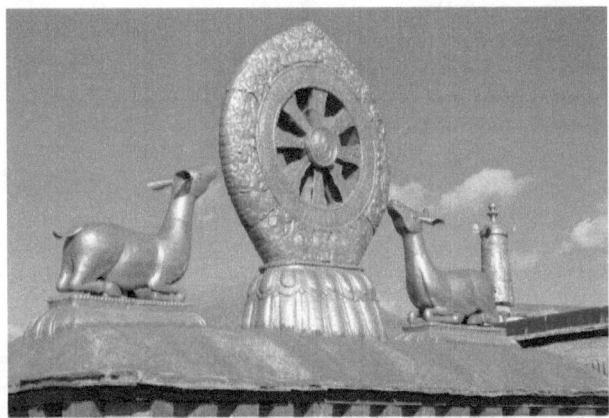

Dharmachakra outside the Tibetan Buddhist temple of Jokhang. It was in a deer park where the Buddha delivered his first teaching after attaining enlightenment. Author's work.

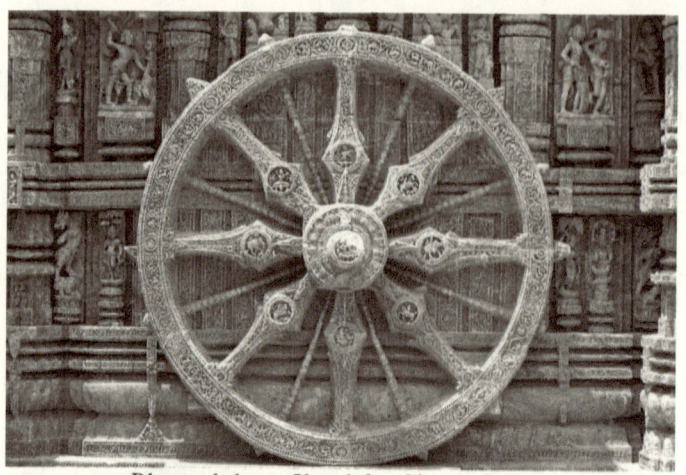

Dharmachakra at Konark Sun Temple, India.[24]

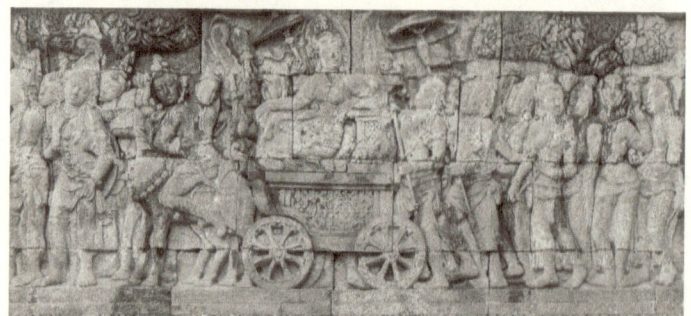

The Buddha's mother, Queen Māyā, being carted to the hills to give birth. Bas relief, Borobudur, central Java. Notice the hallmark character of the cart wheels. Author's work.

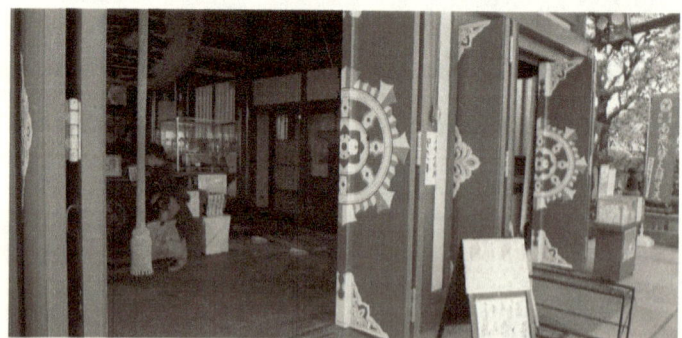

Dharma wheels at the temple of Benzaitendō ("Hall of Saraswati"), Tokyo. Author's work.

Morphology and Meanings

Ashoka's dharmachakra had 24 spokes. Most others, however, have eight. There are many explanations for numeric variety, but several are common.

When a wheel has four spokes, which is rare, the spokes represent Buddhism's Four Noble Truths:

1. All existence is suffering. Our lives are a struggle, and we do not find ultimate happiness or satisfaction in anything we experience. This is the problem of existence.

2. The cause of suffering comes from desire. The natural human tendency is to blame our difficulties on things outside ourselves. But their actual root is found in the mind itself. In particular our tendency to grasp at things puts us at odds with the way life really is.

3. The cessation of suffering comes with the cessation of desire. As we are the ultimate cause of our difficulties, we are also the solution. We cannot change the things that happen to us, but we can change our responses.

4. The Noble Eightfold Path can lead you away from suffering.

When a wheel has eight spokes, the spokes represent the Eightfold Path, which was the historical Buddha's recipe for ending the suffering cycle of birth-death and rebirth. An eight-spoke wheel is the most common form of the dharmachakra in Buddhism.

1. Right Understanding or Perfect Vision
2. Right Resolve or Perfect Emotion
3. Right Speech or Perfect Speech
4. Right Action or Perfect Action
5. Right Livelihood or Perfect Livelihood
6. Right Effort or Perfect Effort
7. Right Mindfulness or Perfect Awareness
8. Right Meditation or Perfect Samadhi

Chapter 7
Buddhist Imagery, Part 1

Images and statues representing the Buddha are extremely diverse. Some depict him as skinny; some, fat. In some, he stands while in others he sits or reclines. Some represent the historical Buddha, Siddhartha Gautama, and others represent a manifestation of a Buddhist deity. Making sense of all the variety would take years of study.

Nevertheless, it is possible to identify several fairly consistent symbolic traits in Buddhist imagery that deserves close attention. Behind each symbol is a story about the Buddha's life and teachings.

The Aniconic Beginning

The historical Buddha, Siddhartha Gautama, lived about 500 BCE. Although his teaching spread rapidly and had immediate effect, followers did not begin creating anthropomorphic (human-like) images of their teacher for several centuries after his death. Instead, they first used aniconic symbols to "suggest" the Buddha's presence. These symbols included footprints, lotus blossoms, the Bodhi tree, empty thrones, and parasols/umbrellas.

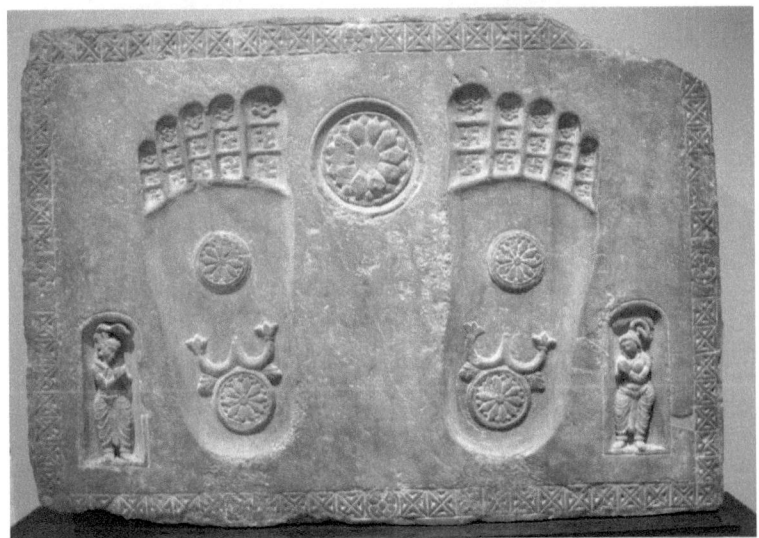

Classic aniconic image representing the Buddha, including footprints and lotus blossoms. Footprints of the Buddha (Buddhapada). 2nd c. CE.[25]

The Buddha's footprints are said to represent how his teachings are "grounded" in the real world. Lotus flowers, which rise above muddy, stagnant water to bloom beautifully, are a metaphor for the human potential to rise above the illusion and suffering of the world through training and practice.

After a long period of study, meditation, and asceticism, Siddhartha Gautama finally sat and meditated below a Bodhi tree in Bodh Gaya, India. Once there, he was assaulted by the demon Mara who tried to distract him with threats and visions of beautiful women. Ultimately, Siddhartha saw the truth of existence and attained enlightenment. He became "the Buddha," the enlightened one. It is the Bodhi tree's association with the site of Buddha's enlightenment that inspires its representation in many early images and carvings.

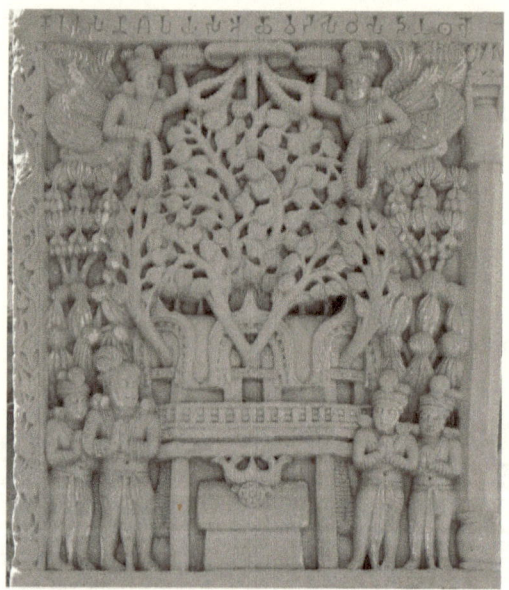

Sculpture of the Bohi tree surrounded by followers at Sanchi, India, 1ˢᵗ century C.E. [26]

The representation of an empty throne is not unique to Buddhism. In fact, it is so common in early Greek and Christian art that there is a word for it: Hetoimasia, meaning "prepared throne." There are many explanations for the significance, but most commentators agree that it is tied to an early discomfort with representing a god in human form. Instead, the god is merely "suggested." As with all aniconic imagery, this kind of suggestion makes possible a broad variety of interpretations.

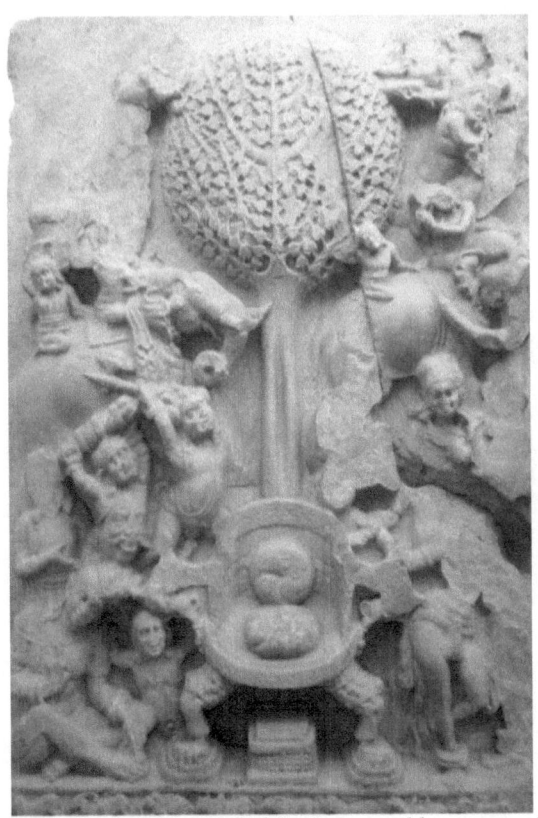

Mara's many demons attacking the Buddha (represented by an empty throne with cushions) under the Bodhi tree.[27]

In Buddhism, an empty throne is often shaded by an umbrella or parasol, which itself suggests the presence of Buddha. Umbrellas have influenced sacred architecture too, appearing on the tops of stupas/pagodas, sometimes in many layers. The three, five, or seven-story pagodas that are common across East Asia may, in fact, be a stylized representation of a many-layered umbrella.

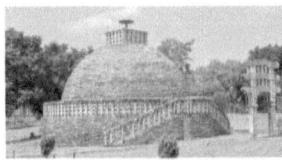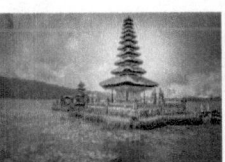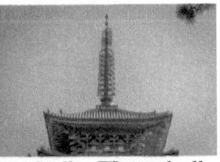

The earliest stupas at Sanchi (left) are topped by a simple umbrella. The umbrella concept may have morphed into pagoda forms found in Bali (middle) and throughout East Asia (right, Japan). Author's works.

Anthropomorphic and Iconic Buddhist Imagery

Although there is scholarly debate, most commentators agree that it was Greek influence that first inspired the production of anthropomorphic images of the Buddha in a place called "Gandhara," corresponding to present-day north-west Pakistan and north-east Afghanistan. From about the 3rd century BCE, Greek rulers such as Alexander the Great (356-323 BCE) held sway in Gandhara.

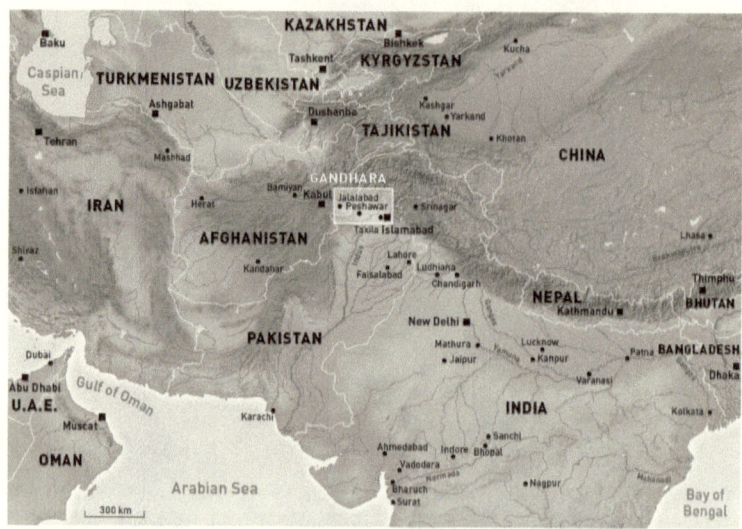

Gandhara map.

Gandharan Buddhist statues often have traits that seem to reflect Greek influence. These traits include Caucasian ethnic features, togas, Doric columns, and even representations of Heracles as protector of the Buddha.

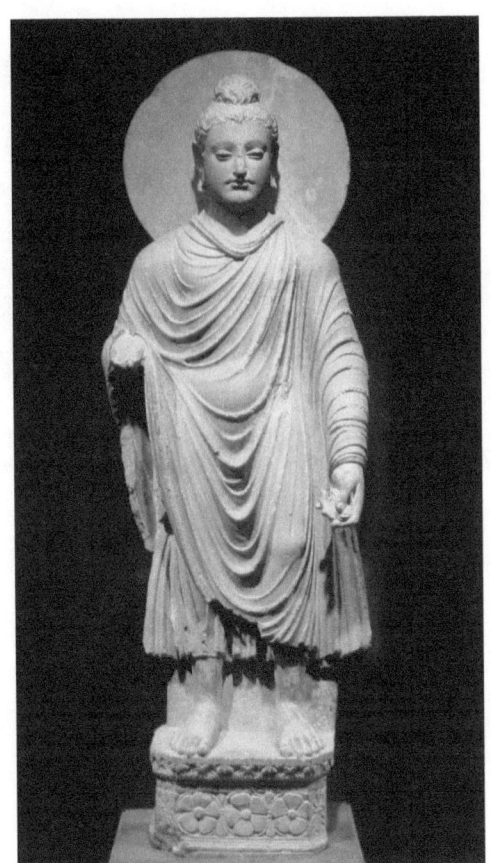

Greco-Buddhist statue of standing Buddha, Gandhara (1st-2nd century). Notice the toga and wavy hair, both typical of Greek motifs.[28]

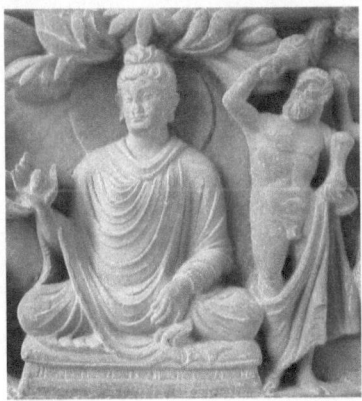

Here, the meditating Buddha is protected by the guardian Vajrapani, who is depicted as Heracles.[29]

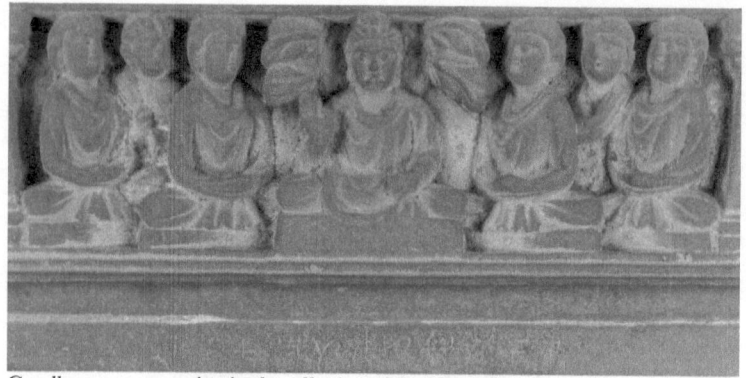

Gandharan stone carving in the collection of the University of Sydney. Note the Greek toga and the leaves that represent the Bodhi tree. Vajrapani is the second figure from the left. The writing at the bottom has not been deciphered. Author's work.

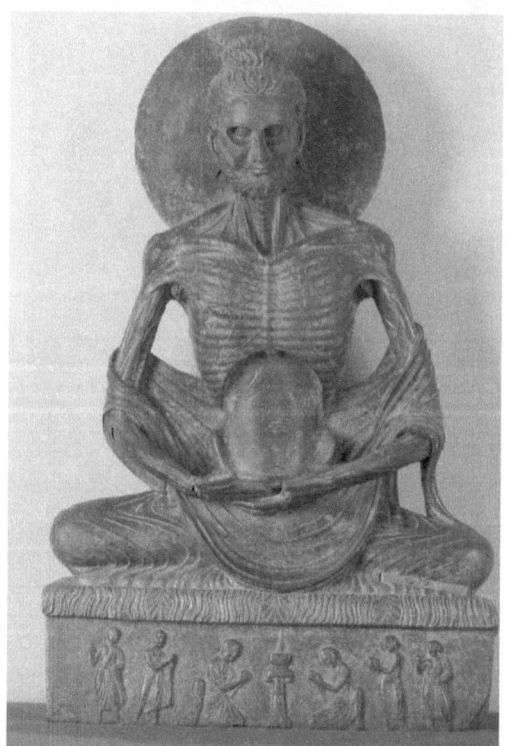

This is perhaps the most famous Gandharan Buddhist statue. It depicts Siddhartha Gautama during his most severe ascetic phase, when it is said he survived on only a single grain of rice a day.[30]

Chapter 8
Buddhist Imagery, Part 2

Once it became widely acceptable to depict the Buddha in human form, from about the dawn of the first millennium, certain iconographic conventions became common. Each is tied to a story about the Buddha's life or enlightenment. Let us examine a few examples before outlining common traits.

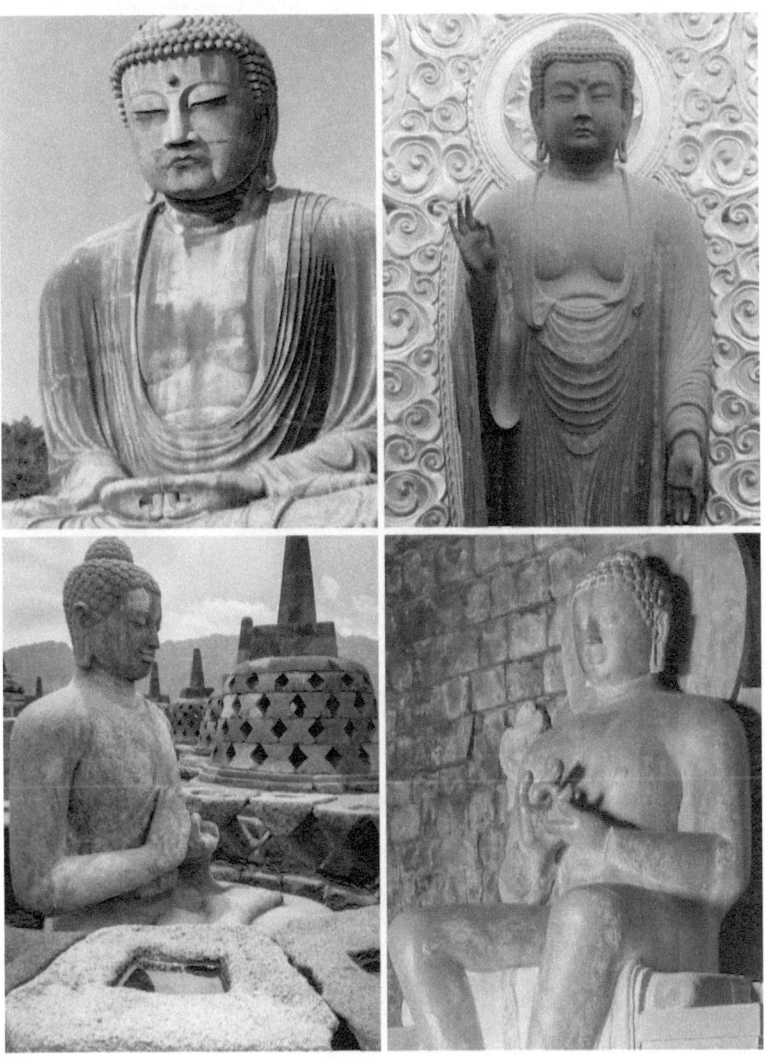

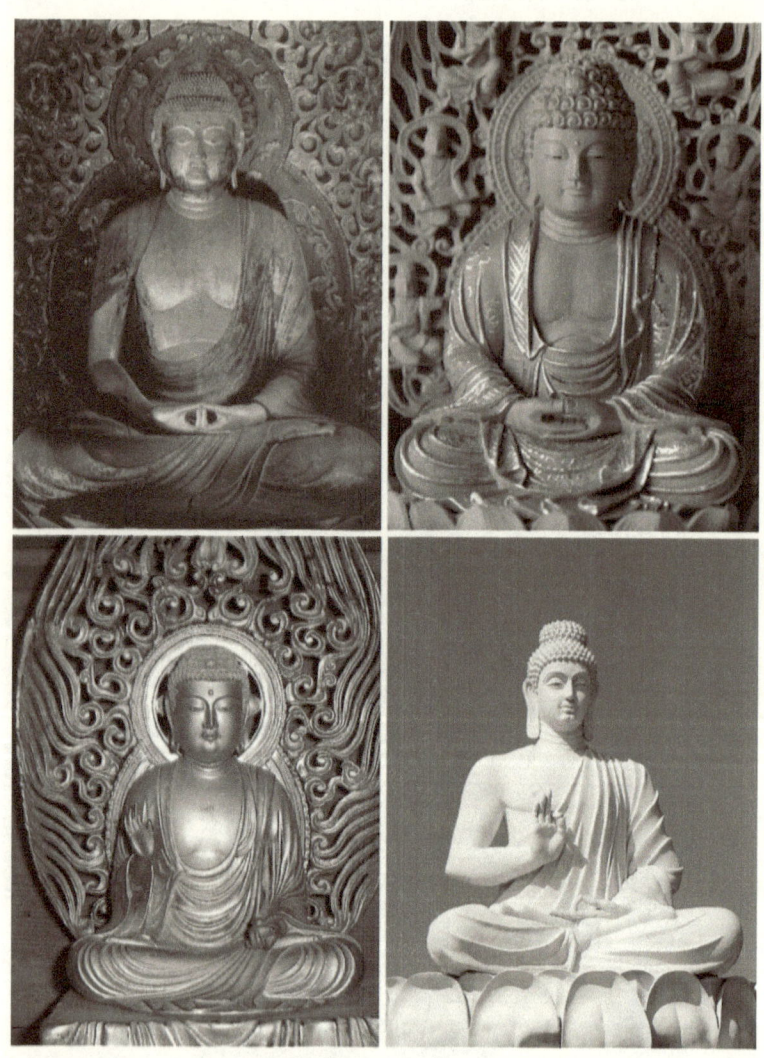

38

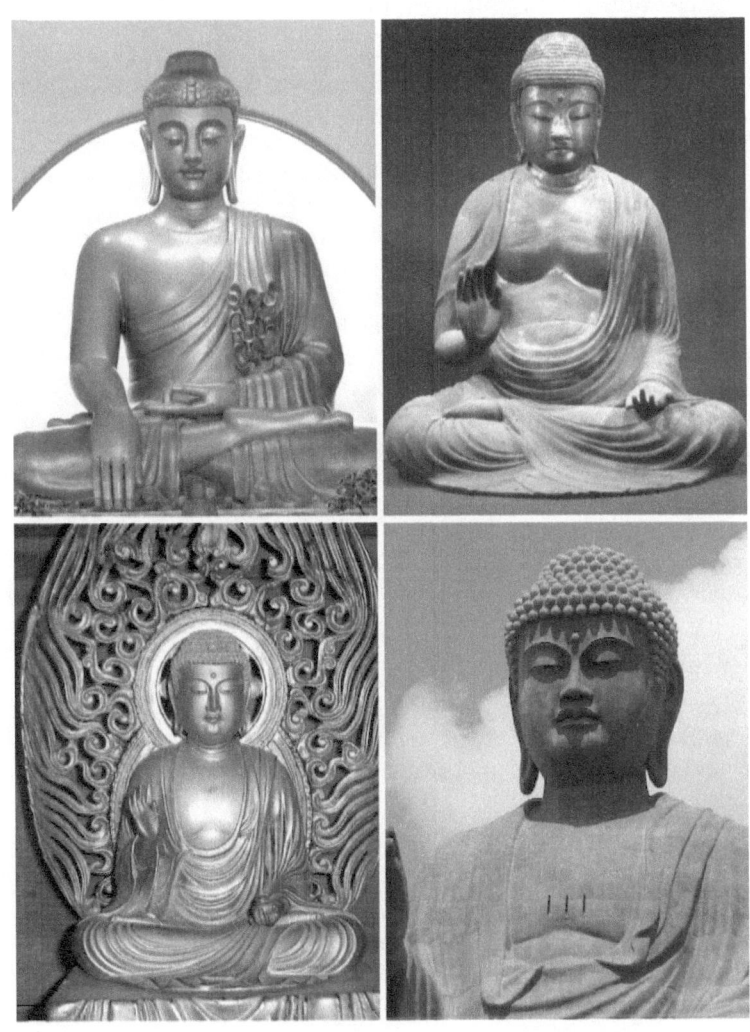

Common Traits

Cranial Bump and "Snail" Curls

Buddha's cranial bump derives from the top knot worn by members of the ruling class. Although the Buddha is said to have shaved his head after going into the forest, he is rarely depicted as bald, except sometimes in Japan. Instead of depicting a top knot or a shaved head, it seems artists have compromised by giving the Buddha a cranial bump. Some scholars claim it represents wisdom.

According to legend, Buddha had to shave his head only once. After that, his regrown hair adhered tightly to his scalp, creating rows of snail-like curls. While standard depictions call for 360 curls, there is great variety based on region. The curls can be large, small, flat, knob like or pointed. Note that the snail pattern is a departure from earlier Gandharan depictions, which use wavy hair.

Third Eye (like a mole on the forehead)

When the Buddha attained enlightenment, he became aware of the true nature of the universe. It was at that very moment when a metaphorical "third eye" opened, allowing him to "see" truth and not be deluded by illusion.

Elongated Ears

Elongated ears are a symbol of Buddha's origin as a prince. In his time, it was standard for a prince to wear heavy ear ornaments that naturally stretched the ear lobes. In places like Thailand, longer ears are considered lucky even today.

Mudra Hand Positions

There are a variety of hand positions, called mudras, used in Indian religions. Each symbolizes a different and unique idea such as "teaching," "warding off ignorance," or "meditation." See the chapter below on mudras for more details.

Lotus Blossom

The Buddha is most frequently depicted as seated or standing upon a lotus blossom. The lotus represents the potential for humanity to rise above the pain and illusion of this world, much like the lotus flower rises out of muddy and stagnant water.

The Mahayana Proliferation of Imagery

Buddhism has three major branches: Theravada, Mahayana, and Vajrayana. In the Mahayana, or "Great Vehicle" tradition, there is a pantheon of Buddhas, servants, guardians, enlightened being (bodhisattva) and incarnations. They all exist to help sentient beings attain salvation and escape from suffering. Due to the variety, Mahayana-inspired art is extremely diverse. In fact, without special training, it can be difficult to distinguish between Buddhas, bodhisattvas, and other members of the pantheon. The explanation of common features touched on in this chapter relates essentially to stock representations of the Buddha.

Chapter 9
The Mudra

A *mudrā* (Sanskrit, "seal," "mark," or "gesture") is a symbolic or ritual gesture common to Hinduism and Buddhism. Most mudras are performed with the hands and fingers. A mudra can be thought of as a spiritual gesture and seal of authenticity employed in the spiritual practice and iconography of Indian religions.

Although there are numerous mudras, six are particularly common and can be found across Asia. Understanding mudras makes it possible to interpret what Buddhist images are trying to convey. They show what the Buddha is "doing" in the image.

Dhyana Mudra: Meditation

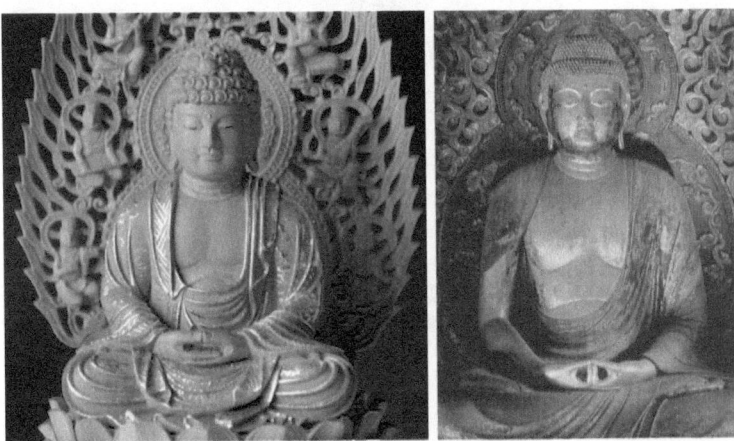

Dhyana mudra signifies meditation. Both hands are in the lap with palms upward. The right hand is usually on top of the left. Touching knuckles and thumbs is another version of the same mudra.

Bhumisparsa Mudra: Calling the Earth to Witness

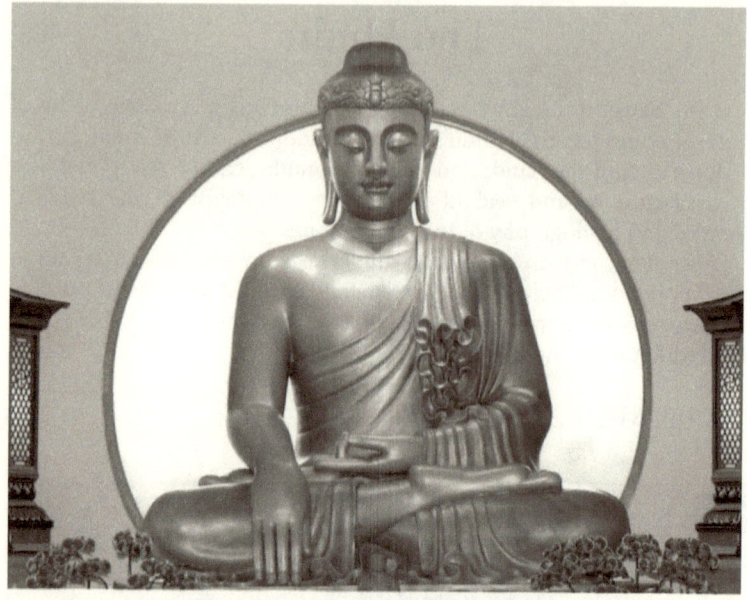

Under the Bodhi tree, Siddhartha was subjected to many temptations by the evil Mara, who bombarded him with demons, monsters, violent storms and three seductive daughters. The Buddha remained focused. Then, at the moment of his enlightenment, he gently touched the ground with his right hand and "called the earth to witness" his remarkable merit and achievement. Bhumisparsa symbolizes enlightenment as well as steadfastness (imperturbability).

Abhaya Mudra: Imparting Reassurance

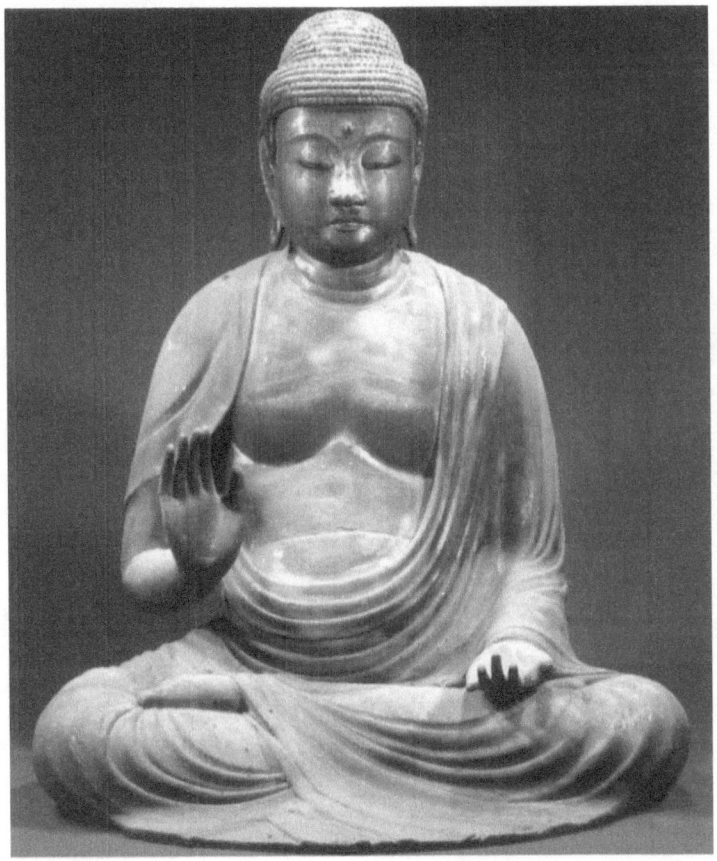

Abhaya mudra is made with the hand raised and the palm facing outwards. It is the gesture of reassurance and safety, which dispels fear and accords divine protection and bliss. One might think of it as the Buddha saying, "everything's going to be okay." A different explanation claims that it represents the Buddha holding ignorance and suffering at bay ("stop").

Vitarka Mudra: Teaching

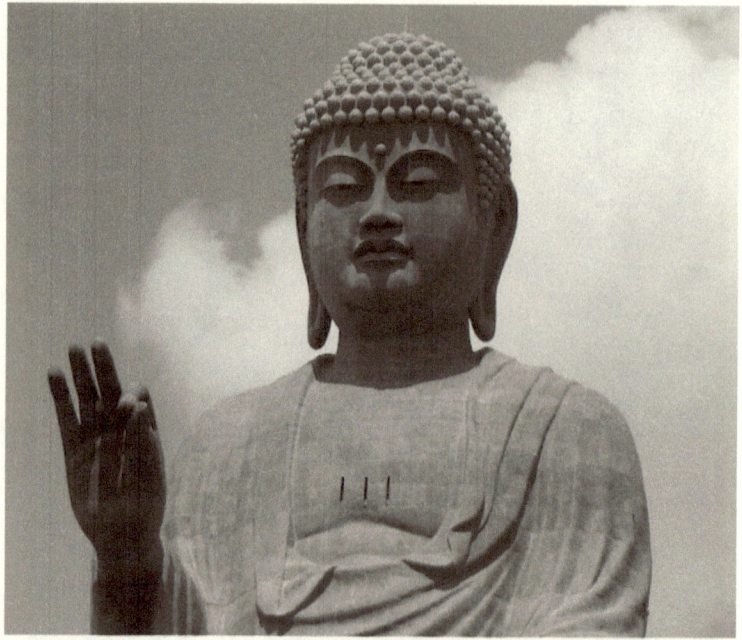

    The vitarka mudra has a great number of variations. In most cases, the right hand is raised with palm facing the viewer. The index finger and thumb touch to make a gentle circle. The vitarka mudra symbolizes "teaching the Dharma."

Dharmachakra Mudra: Turning the Wheel of Dharma

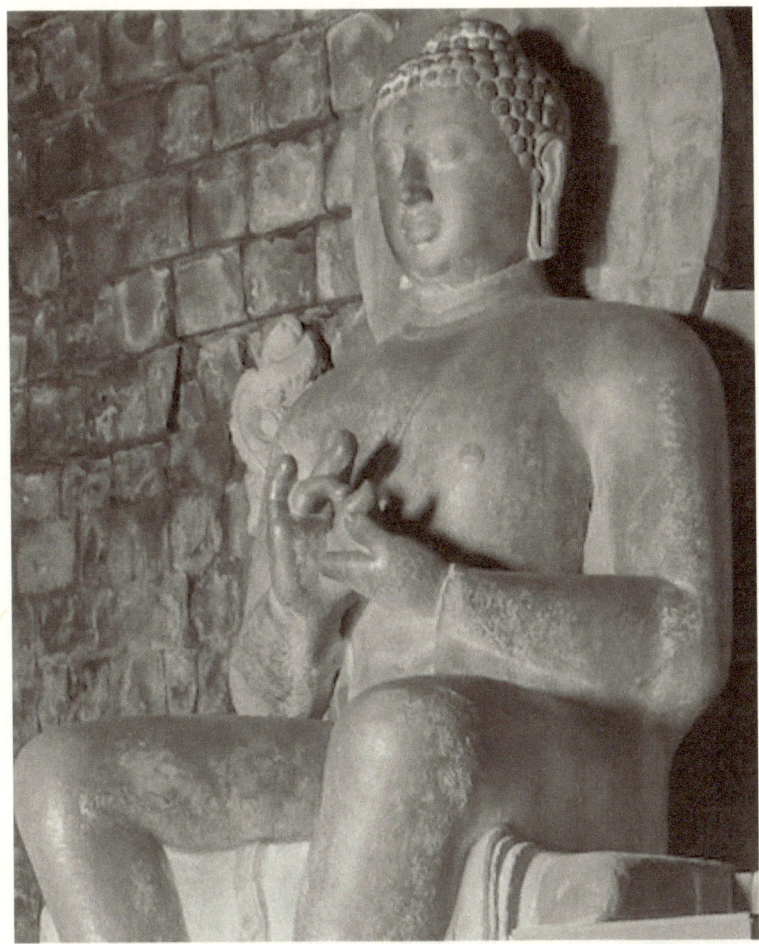

In the dharmachakra mudra, the fingers of the left hand rest against the palm of the right hand as if turning a wheel made by the index finger and thumb of the right hand. It signifies the Buddha's first teaching at the deer park in Sarnath, India. According to legend, it was on that occasion when he first "turned the wheel" of the Dharma.

Varada Mudra: Charity

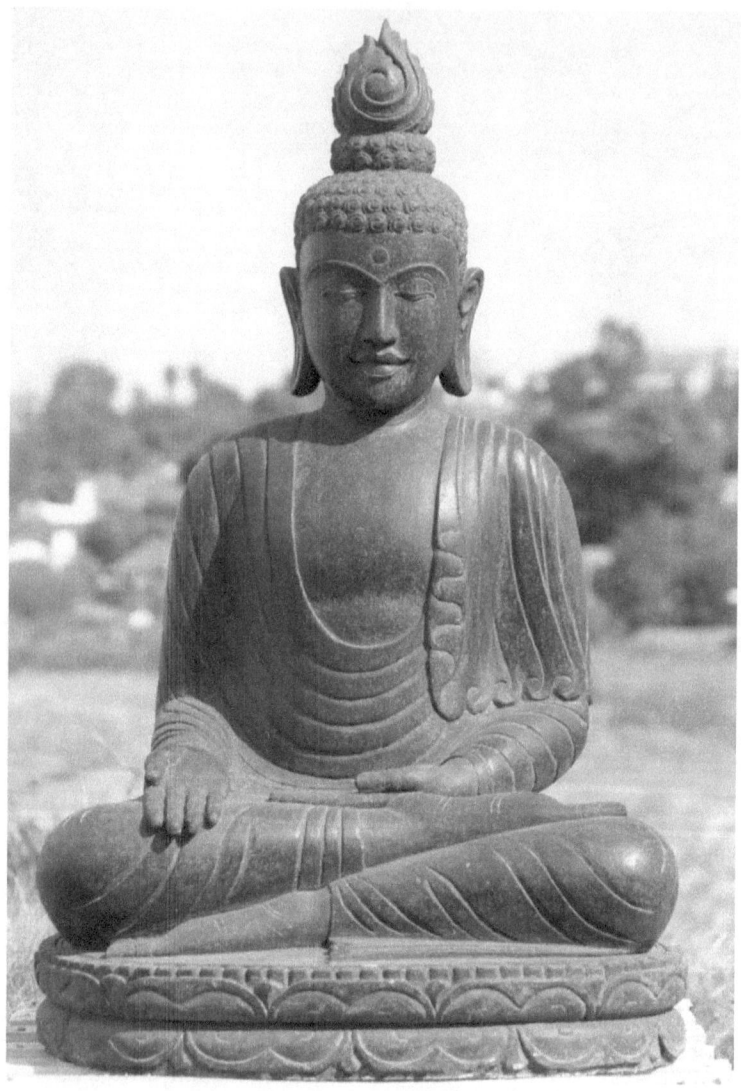

The hand lowered with the palm facing outward is the gesture of "bestowing blessings" or "giving charity."

Chapter 10
The Hindu Trimūrti

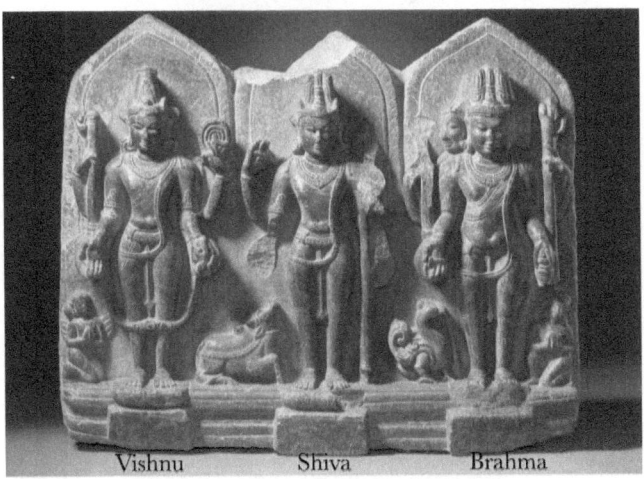

Vishnu   Shiva   Brahma

The Trimūrti, meaning "three forms," comprises the triple deities of supreme divinity in Hinduism, including Brahma, Vishnu and Shiva. Brahma's sacred duty was the original creation of the world and all creatures. His name should not be confused with Brahman, which is the supreme force present in all things. Vishnu is the preserver of the universe, while Shiva's role is to destroy it in order to re-create. Brahma is the least worshipped god in Hinduism today. There are only two temples in India devoted to him, compared with the many thousands devoted to the other two.

Brahma the Creator

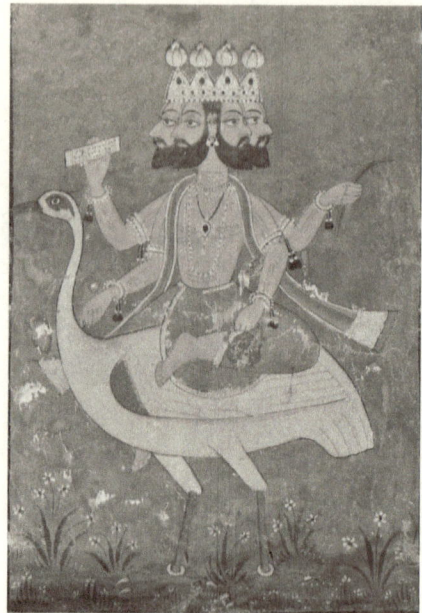

Brahma the Creator portrait.[31]

Brahma can be most readily identified as the god with four faces and four arms. He is accompanied by a swan or goose. The animals that accompany Hindu deities are called *"vahana,"* a Sanskrit word that means "vehicle." The similarity between the Sanskrit and English words is not coincidental. The two languages have many terms in common due to shared origin in Indo-Aryan culture.

Each of Brahma's four mouths are said to have produced the four Vedas, the most sacred books of Hinduism. Teachings claim that Brahma's cosmic body was divided up when creating the world, with different sections becoming different classes (*varnas*) of society.

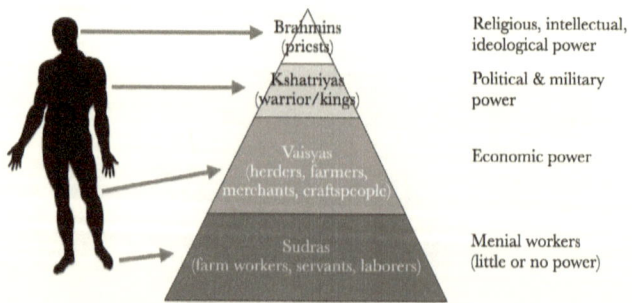

Brahma's creation of the Vedic varnas. Author's work.

Brahma's chief consort is Saraswati, who is widely revered in Southeast Asia and Japan. In Japan she is called "Benzaiten."

Vishnu the Preserver

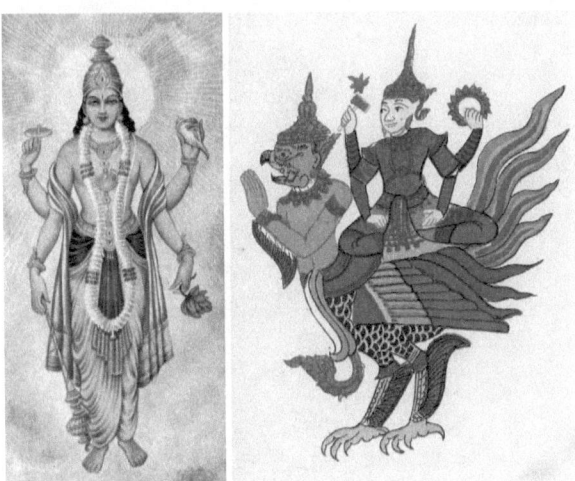

Vishnu is usually depicted as having dark blue, blue-gray or black skin and four arms. He holds a lotus flower (*padma*) in his lower left hand, a mace (*Kaumodaki gada*) in his lower right hand, a conch (*Panchajanya shankha*) in his upper left hand and a discus (*Sudarshana Chakra*) in his upper right hand.

Vishnu's *vahana* is garuda, a sacred, eagle-like bird. Garuda features prominently in the iconography of Southeast Asia, including the national symbol of Indonesia.

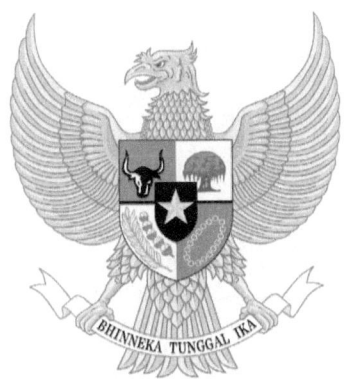

The official crest of Indonesia features Garuda.

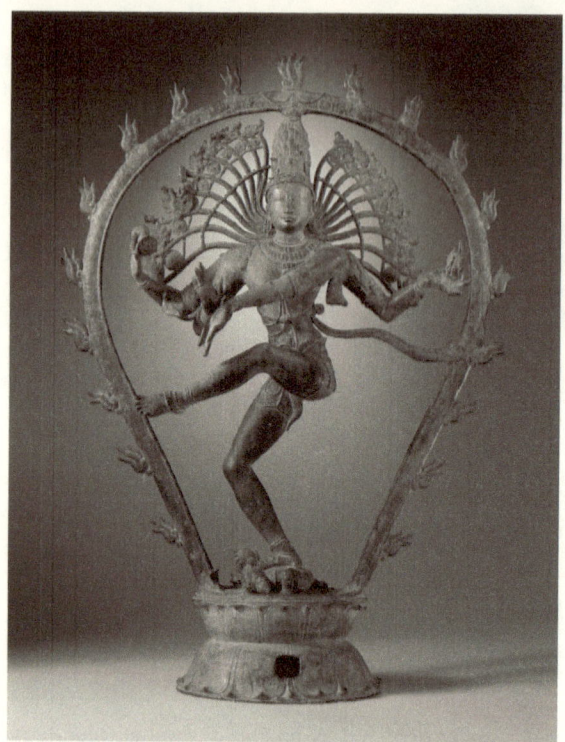

Shiva, the Lord of the Dance (Shiva Nataraja), 10th c.[32]

Shiva is the supreme being within Shaivism ("Shiva worship"), one of the major traditions within Hinduism. He is known as "the Destroyer," the supreme being who creates, protects and transforms the universe. In Indian philosophy, creating and destroying are often considered two parts of a single continuum. That is why Shiva plays a key role in creation despite Brahma being "the Creator." Creation can only be achieved through destruction, an Indian idea that long predates Newtonian laws about the conservation of energy and mass. In the bronze statue pictured above, Shiva (called Shiva Nataraja) is dancing the world into destruction, an act that itself brings new worlds into existence. Deploying a visual device that is extremely common in Hindu-Buddhist imagery, he is trampling the figure of "ignorance" (Apasmāra) under foot.

Shiva is often shown seated upon a tiger skin, garlanded with a snake. He carries a trident, symbolic of his tripartite role as creator, preserver and destroyer. Shiva's *vahana* is Nandi the bull.

Chapter 11
Lotus, Pearl, and Vajra

Lotus

The lotus belongs to a set of "eight auspicious symbols" in Indian religions, called the Ashtamangala. Other symbols in the set include the dharmachakra (dharma wheel) and the umbrella or parasol.

The lotus is central to the symbolism of Indian religions, including Hinduism, Buddhism, Sikhism, and Jainism. In Hinduism, the gods Lakshmi, Vishnu, and Brahma are closely associated with the lotus, which is an example of divine beauty and purity. The blossom's growth out of (transcendence from) a muddy and stagnant pond symbolizes a benign spiritual promise.

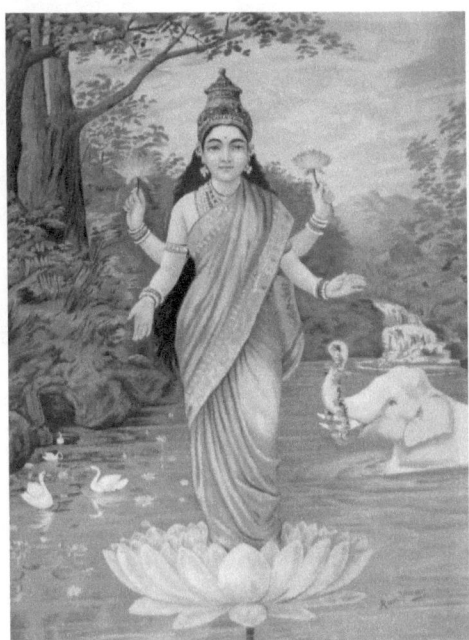

Lakshmi depicted standing on and holding lotuses.[33]

In Buddhist symbolism, the lotus represents purity of the body, speech and mind. Although it is rooted in the mud, the lotus blossoms on long stalks as if floating above the muddy waters of attachment and desire. It is also symbolic of detachment because drops of water easily bead off its petals.

The Buddha and Buddhist deities are frequently depicted as seated or standing on a lotus. According to legend, Siddhartha Gautama was born with the ability to walk. Everywhere he stepped, lotus flowers bloomed. It is for this reason that lotuses often appear embedded within Buddhist "footprint" imagery.

The Pearl

The pearl is a symbol of perfection and incorruptibility. Its luster inspires an association with the moon. Buried within the oyster shell, the pearl can represent hidden knowledge. Many philosophies of Asia (Buddhism, Taoism, Hinduism) relate the "flaming pearl" to wisdom. A comparison can be made with the way Western cultures speak of the "pearl of wisdom."

Another interpretation is comparable to the symbolism of the lotus. Like the lotus, the pearl originates from imperfection when a grain of sand gets caught within an oyster. After years of development—which can be compared to religious practice—it becomes smooth, pure and beautiful.

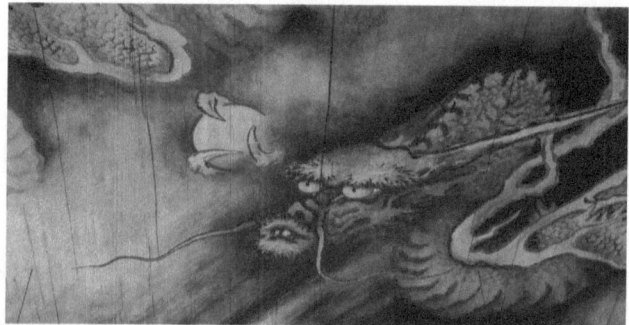

Pearls frequently appear in imagery involving dragons such as this monochrome ceiling painting at the temple of Tōfukuji in Kyoto, Japan. Author's work.

Vajra

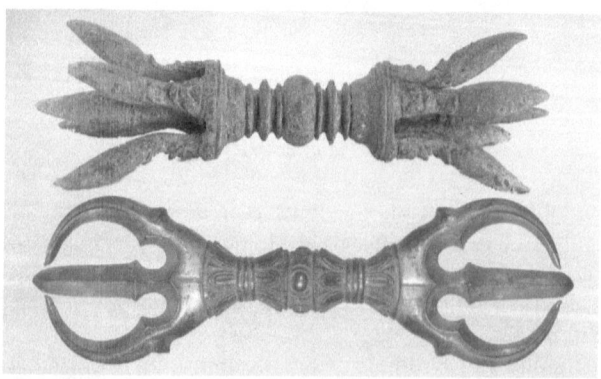

The Sanskrit word "vajra" means both diamond (an indestructible substance) and thunderbolt (an unstoppable force). It is the weapon of Indra, the Indian deity of rain and thunder, and is used symbolically in the traditions of Buddhism, Jainism and Hinduism, often to represent firmness of spirit and spiritual power.

One of the earliest enlightened beings (bodhisattva) to be represented alongside the Buddha was Vajrapani, the "one with a vajra in his hand." He is the Buddha's guide and protector.

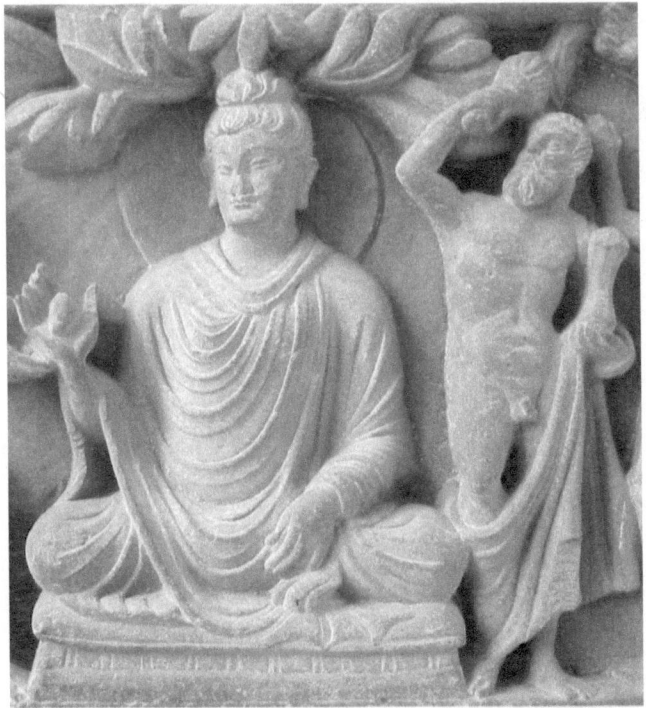

In this early Gandharan relief, Vajrapani closely resembles Heracles of Greek mythology. He carries the vajra "thunderbolt" in his left hand.[34]

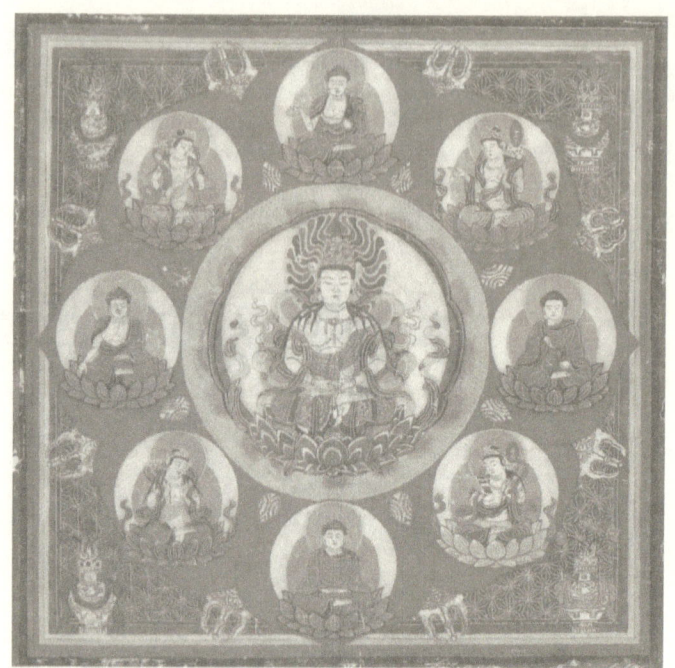

Eight vajras emanate from the center of the womb mandala.

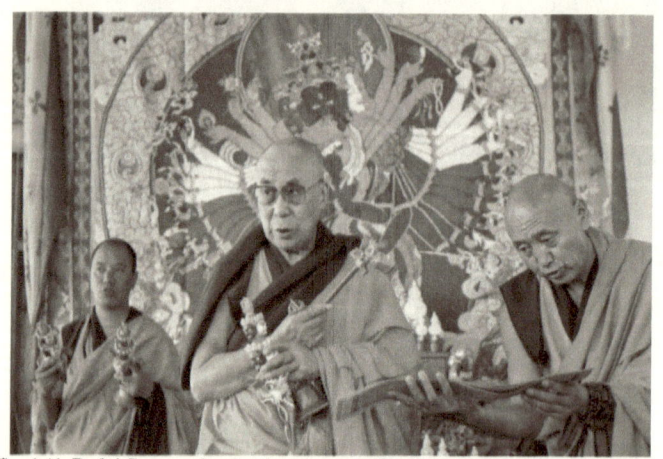

The 14th Dalai Lama often holds a vajra in his right hand and a bell in his left hand when performing rituals.[35]

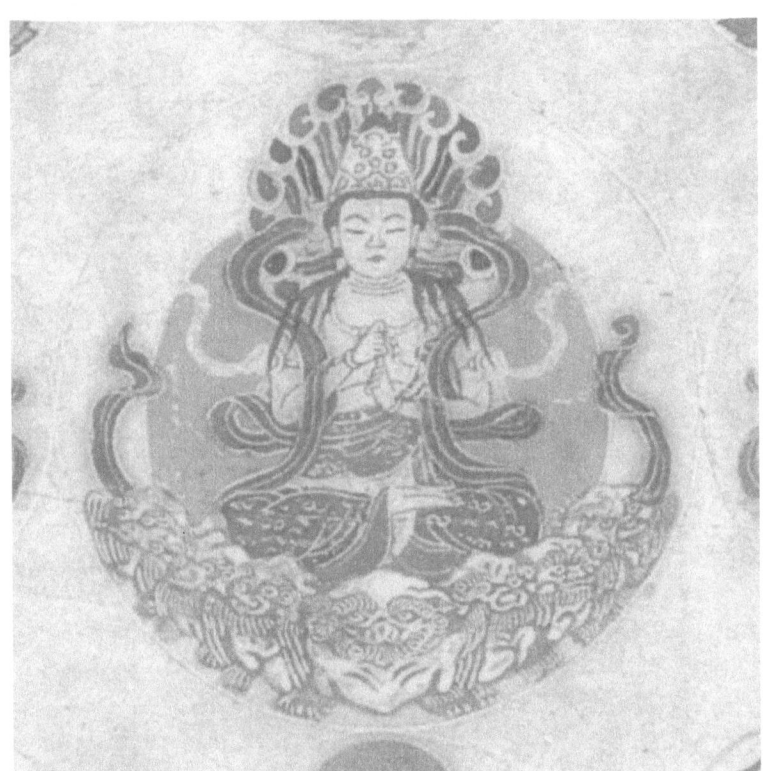

In this image from the Diamond Mandala, the deity is forming the "vajra mudra" with his hands.

Section 2
Hindu-Buddhist Cosmology

At times and in places where kings justified their rule on sacred grounds ("I am an avatar of Shiva" or "I am the reborn Buddha!"), cosmology became extremely important. Cosmology is simply an explanation for the structure of the universe, physically and metaphysically. It helps people order living beings, objects, and ideas in a quasi-physical way. As a simple example, Judeo-Christian cosmology has three primary realms: hell, the world of the living, and heaven. The cosmology of most aboriginal Australians includes the "dreamtime," which is a place, a time, and a metaphorical state of being.

Throughout the premodern world (and even sometimes today), many leaders thought of their individual realms as the center of the universe, with their temples and palaces constituting the very core. We see this in China, whose name literally means "the middle kingdom" (中国). In Europe, Jerusalem was long considered the center of the world because it was the birthplace of Christ.

Chapter 12
Mount Meru

Mt. Meru is the sacred, five-peaked mountain of Hindu, Jain, and Buddhist cosmology. It is considered the center of the physical, metaphysical, and spiritual universes. Many Hindu and Buddhist temples have been built as symbolic representations of Mt. Meru and the mountain is frequently associated with important stupas and pagodas. Mandalas are often interpreted as reflections of the sacred mountain.

According to Indian legend, the god Indra "pegged" the floating primordial mound to the bottom of the Cosmic Ocean, thus "fixing" or "stabilizing" the universe.

In most cultures, Mt. Meru is a mythical place. It is merely a paradigm or part of an idealized picture of the universe rather than an actual mountain. Someone might symbolically strive for it or build something to represent it, but they will never dream of actually ever visiting. In other cultures, however, Mt. Meru is an actual place, a mountain that is looked to as the center of the cosmos. This is true in Java, Indonesia. Echoing the story of Indra, the island's tallest mountain, Mt. Sumeru, is considered the "nail of the world." It is meant to hold the island in place and, by association, give stability to the world. Judging from the frequency and severity of earthquakes in Java, one might think that it is not secured very well!

Mt. Meru can have serious political significance. For a king to call his palace or capital the center of the universe is fairly normal in many premodern cultures around the world ("all roads lead to Rome"; "Middle Kingdom," etc.). In Asia, kings often leveraged the notion of Mt. Meru to help legitimize their rule. By saying "my palace or temple is Mt. Meru," they instantly centralized themselves, their capital, and their kingdom within an idealized universal structure, a cosmology. They *became* the center of the universe!

Traits

Although there are various descriptions of Mt. Meru across different cultures, several traits are fairly consistent. First, it is said to have five peaks and to be shaped like an hourglass. The top and base are extremely broad, with the mountain's profile dramatically narrowing at the middle. The square base is surrounded by a square, "cosmic ocean." The ocean is in turn surrounded by a wall of mountains, which is in turn surrounded by a sea. There are seven seas and seven surrounding mountain-walls, each diminishing in width and height.

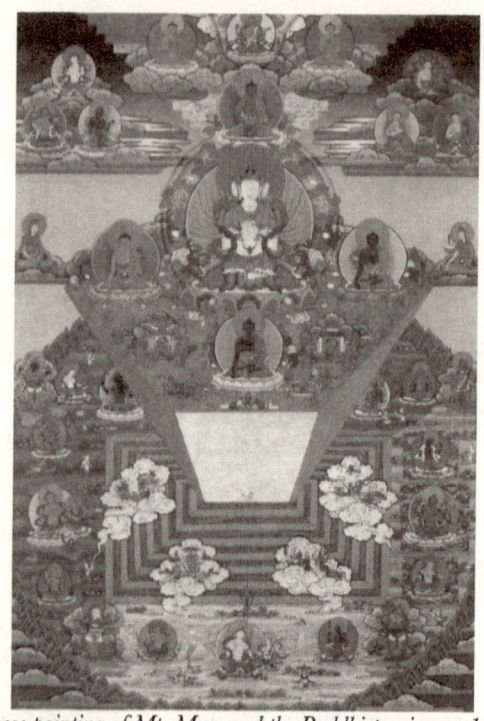

Bhutanese painting of Mt. Meru and the Buddhist universe, 19th c.[36]

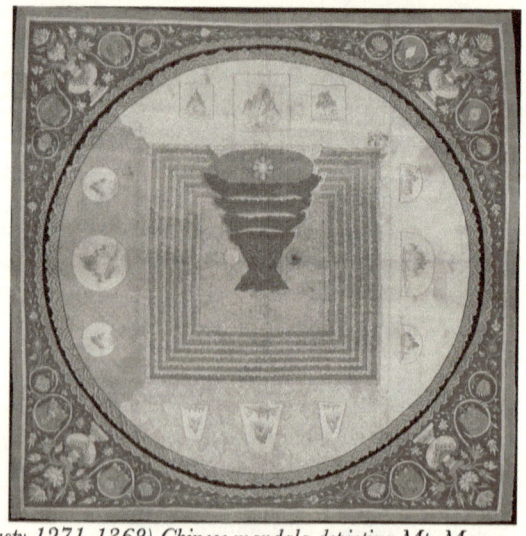

Yuan dynasty 1271-1368) Chinese mandala depicting Mt. Meru as an inverted pyramid topped by a lotus.[37]

In Southeast Asia, the kings who claimed to be sacred rulers with kingdoms located at the center of the universe, often built palaces with five great spires. We can see this today in places like Angkor (Cambodia) and Prambanan (Java, Indonesia).

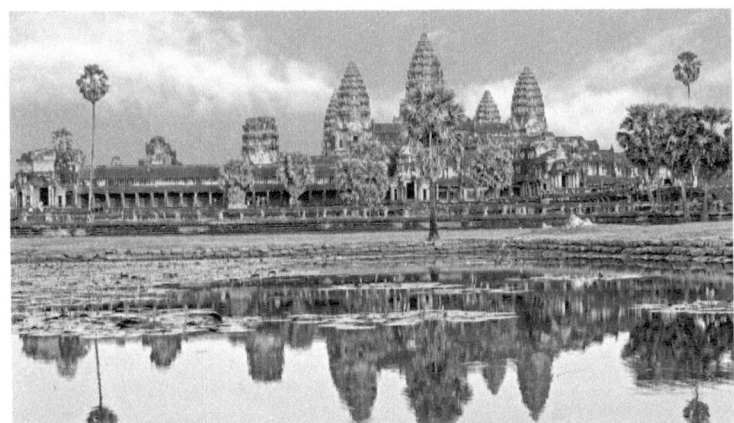

Angkor Wat, Cambodia. Author's work.

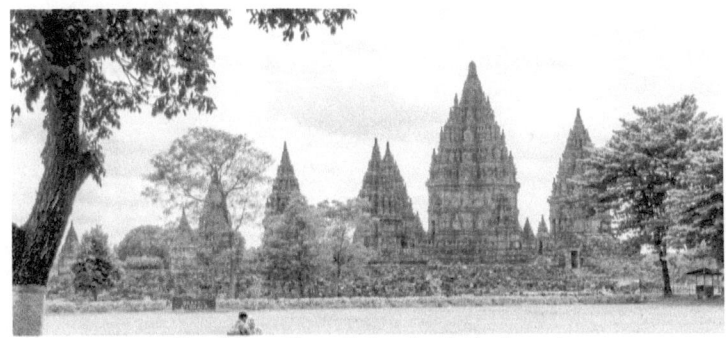

Prambanan, Java, Indonesia. Author's work.

Chapter 13
The Stupa or Pagoda

At the time of the Buddha, it was already common for revered spiritual leaders to be buried within mound tombs called stupas. Legend holds that the historical Buddha requested his own remains to be interred within a similar domed structure Over time, the Buddha's followers divided up the remains and created more stupas as reliquaries. Many believers and practitioners visited the stupas to pay their respects to the enlightened one and to engage in rituals thought to grant merit.

Eventually, a distinct architectural style emerged. Stupas in India were stone, domed structures with a square balustrade at the top. The peak was often topped by an umbrella. Surrounding the dome was a low wall that was often ornately decorated with images from Hindu-Buddhist tales and the life of the Buddha. Practitioners would pass into this walled area and circumambulate the stupa clockwise to accrue merit.

Ashoka the Great (stupa builder)

After Ashoka the Great unified most of India in about 268 BCE, he began an ambitious project to build 80,000 stupas to distribute Buddhist relics across his realm and beyond. The project was closely associated with Ashoka's concurrent construction of pillars carved with Buddhist-inspired teachings, capped by lion capitals.

The Stupa at Sanchi, central India, is Ashoka's oldest and most celebrated creation. It is considered the paradigmatic model of the Indian-style stupa.

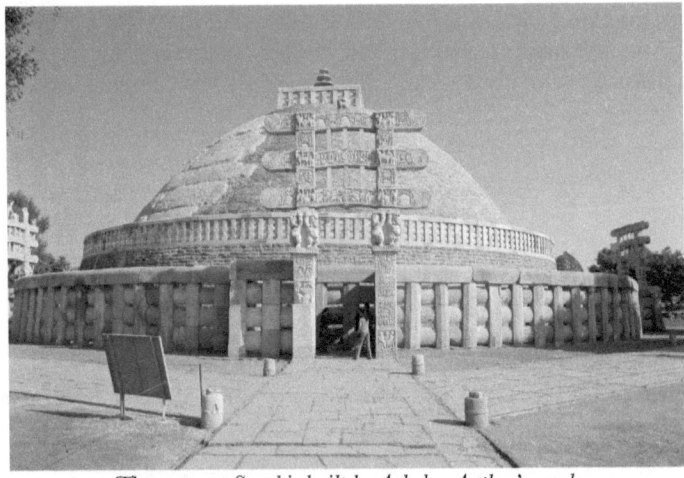

The stupa at Sanchi, built by Ashoka. Author's work.

Political Meanings

The pagoda's meaning could sometimes be political. As sacred sites, pagodas were associated with the notion of Mt. Meru. The ruler who built a great stupa was legitimized by association with the universe's sacred geography and, through that association, became an active agent in maintaining the order of the universe. Rulers sought to forge an "anthropocosmic" relationship: that is, a relationship between the realm of people ("anthro") and the realm of the gods or heaven ("cosmic"). This idea was very likely what motivated Ashoka's building projects as well as those of countless later rulers across the region.

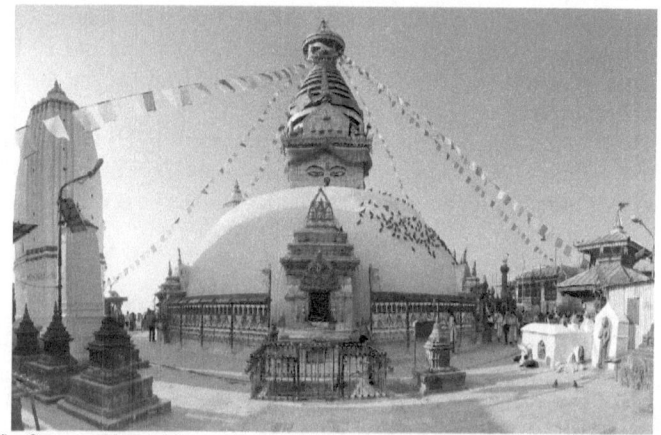

The Swayambhunath stupa in Kathmandu, Nepal. Notice how the basic Sanchi model has been modified. Author's work.

Pagodas

As Buddhism spread across Asia, the shape of the stupa changed. In East Asia, the structures are generally called "pagodas," but stupas and pagodas are essentially the same thing, merely with different shapes.

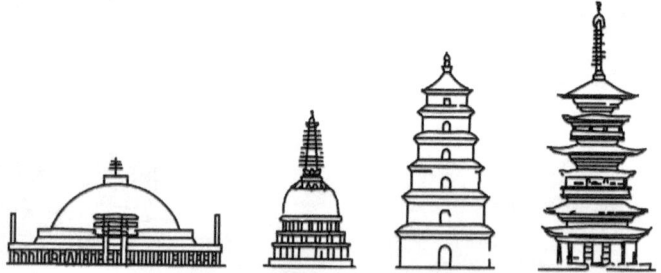

This graphic is a simplified representation of the evolution of stupas. From left to right: Indian, Southeast Asian, Chinese, Japanese. Author's work.

In China

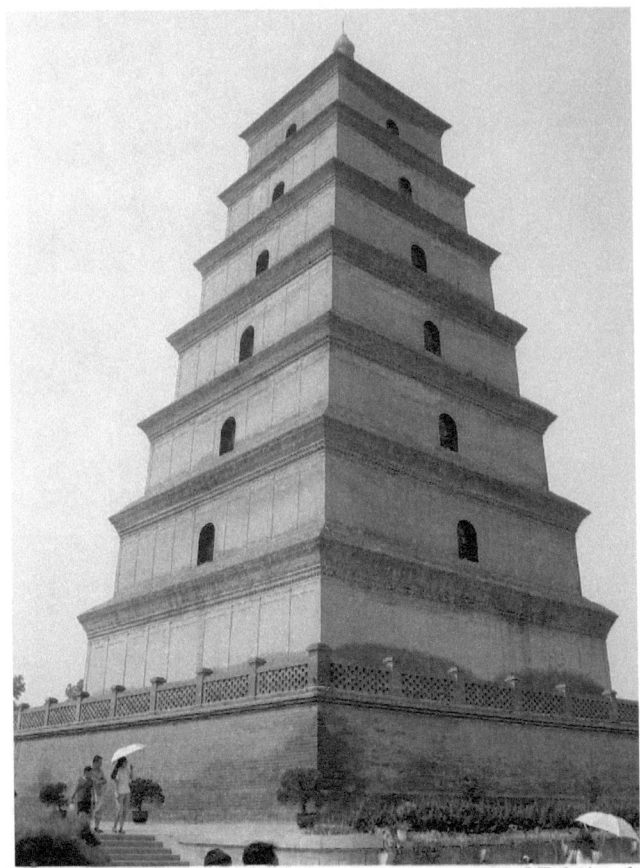

The Giant Wild Goose Pagoda of Xi'an, built in the year 652 CE during the Tang Dynasty, when the city was named Chang'an. Author's work.

In Southeast Asia

In Southeast Asia—particularly places like Myanmar and Thailand—stupas took on a strong conical shape.

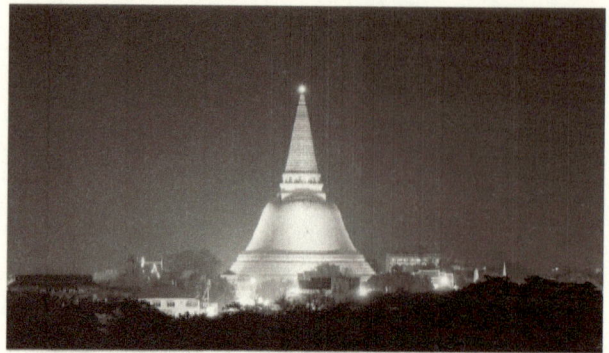

The Phra Pathommachedi stupa in Thailand. Author's work.

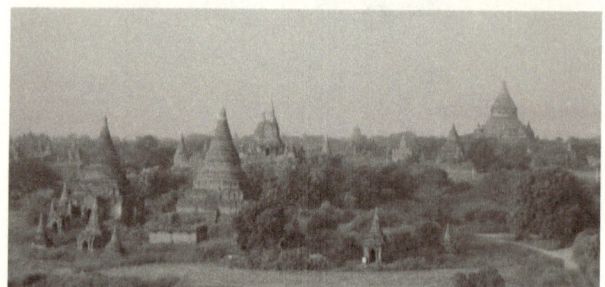

The famous stupas of Bagan, Myanmar. Author's work.

In cases such as Borobudur in central Java, we find that stupas are brought together into composites to create structures that are themselves stupas. In this way, Borobudur is a hologram of a stupa: a stupa made from countless smaller stupas.

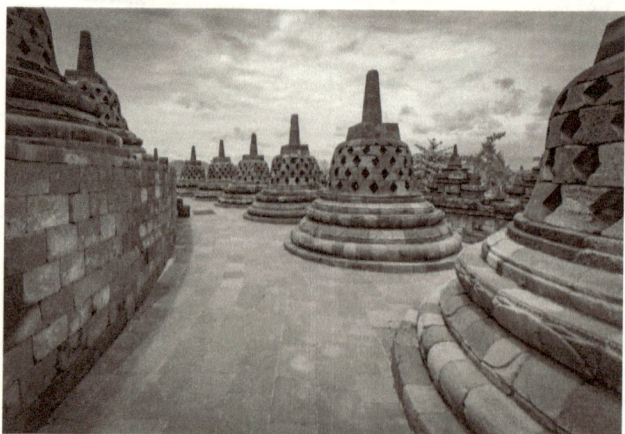

Borobudur, central Java. Author's work.

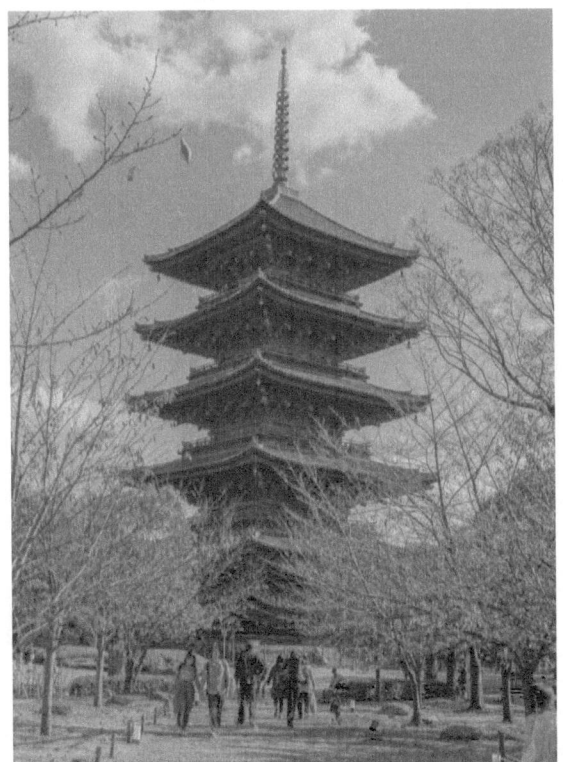

A five-storied pagoda at the temple of Ninnaji, Kyoto. Author's work.

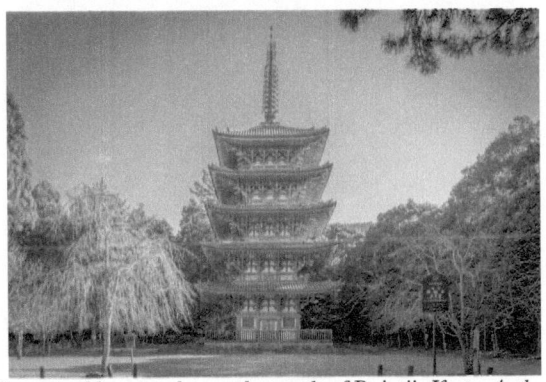

One of Japan's oldest pagodas, at the temple of Daigoji, Kyoto. Author's work.

Notes

[1] Campion, Mukti Jain, "How the world loved the swastika - until Hitler stole it." https://www.bbc.com/news/magazine-29644591

[2] Courtesy of Exekias, creative commons attribution 2.0. https://commons.wikimedia.org/wiki/File:Greek_Silver_Stater_of_Corinth.jpg

[3] Courtesy of Dr. Avishai Teacher, public domain. https://commons.wikimedia.org/wiki/File:Swastikas_in_byzantine_Church_in_Shavei-Zion,_Israel.jpg

[4] Courtesy of Saamiblog: http://saamiblog.blogspot.com/

[5] Courtesy of InOutPeaceProject. https://www.flickr.com/people/93485852@N05

[6] Property of Yale University Library, public domain. https://artgallery.yale.edu/collections/objects/112686

[7] Guénon, René and Fohr, Samuel D., "Symbols of Sacred Science," *Sophia Perennis* (2004): pp. 64-67, 113-117.

[8] *The Conversation*, "How Nazis twisted the swastika into a symbol of hate." 1 Sep. 2017. https://theconversation.com/how-nazis-twisted-the-swastika-into-a-symbol-of-hate-83020

[9] The Holocaust Museum, "The Origins of the Swastika." https://encyclopedia.ushmm.org/content/en/article/history-of-the-swastika

[10] James G. Lochtefeld (2002). *The Illustrated Encyclopedia of Hinduism*: A-M. The Rosen Publishing Group. pp. 147, entry for Chidambaram.

[11] Property of the Los Angeles County Museum of Art, public domain. https://collections.lacma.org/node/240893

[12] Courtesy of Shahnoor Habib Munmun, creative commons. https://en.wikipedia.org/wiki/Yoni#/media/File:Shiva_Lingam_with_Gauripatta_at_Mahasthangarh_Museum.jpg

[13] Courtesy of Nevil Zaveri, creative commons. https://en.wikipedia.org/wiki/Lingam#/media/File:A_river_and_decorated_Shiva_linga_pooja,_Hindu_rituals.jpg

[14] Sarah Welch, creative commons. https://en.wikipedia.org/wiki/Kama_Sutra#/media/File:3rd_or_4th_century_CE_Kamasutra,_Vatsyayana,_13th-century_Jayamangala_commentary_of_Yashodhara,_Bendall_purchase_1885CE_in_Nepal,_Sanskrit,_Devanagari.jpg

[15] These images are in the public domain and widely available.

[16] Courtesy of Jakub Hałun, GNU free documentation license. https://commons.wikimedia.org/wiki/File:20090528_Beijing_Lions_Forbidden_City_8006.jpg

[17] For more details see OnMarkProductions. http://www.onmarkproductions.com/html/shishi.shtml

[18] Google Arts & Culture, "The Surprising History of Dragons." https://artsandculture.google.com/story/CgJyM6TaZ5rRJg

[19] Courtesy of Mindy Landeck.

[20] Courtesy of Mindy Landeck.

[21] Property of the Metropolitan Museum of Art, New York City, public domain. https://www.metmuseum.org/blogs/now-at-the-met/2014/peacocks-and-dragons

[22] Doré, Henri (1917), *Researches into Chinese Superstitions*. M. Kennelly, D. J. Finn, and L. F. McGreat, trs. T'usewei. Ch'eng-wen reprint 1966: p. 681.

[23] From Amaravathi village, Guntur district, Andhra Pradesh (India). Preserved in Guimet Museum, Paris. WikiCommons image. https://upload.wikimedia.org/wikipedia/commons/7/75/Indian_relief_from_Amaravati%2C_Guntur._Preserved_in_Guimet_Museum.jpg

[24] Courtesy of saamiblog, creative commons. https://www.flickr.com/photos/28772513@N07/7334606504

[25] Property of Yale University Library, public domain. https://artgallery.yale.edu/collections/objects/112686

[26] Courtesy of Biswarup Ganguly, creative commons. https://en.wikipedia.org/wiki/Bodhi_Tree#/media/File:Pipal_tree_temple_of_Bodh_Gaya_depicted_in_Sanchi_Stupa_1_Eastern_Gateway.jpg

[27] Author unknown. Wikicommons. https://commons.wikimedia.org/wiki/File:MaraAssault.jpg

[28] Courtesy of Tokyo National Museum, public domain. https://upload.wikimedia.org/wikipedia/commons/b/b8/Gandhara_Buddha_%28tnm%29.jpeg

[29] Property of the British Museum, public domain photograph. https://upload.wikimedia.org/wikipedia/commons/3/3e/Buddha-Vajrapani-Herakles.JPG

[30] Property of Lahore Museum, Lahore, Pakistan. From Google Arts & Culture.

[31] Property of the Museum of Fine Arts, Boston, public domain. https://collections.mfa.org/objects/149171

[32] Property of the Los Angeles County Museum of Art, public domain. https://collections.mfa.org/objects/149171

[33] Raja Ravi Varma public domain. https://commons.wikimedia.org/wiki/File:Raja_Ravi_Varma,_Goddess_Lakshmi,_1896.jpg

[34] Property of the British Museum, public domain photograph.
https://commons.wikimedia.org/wiki/File:Buddha-Vajrapani-Herakles.JPG
[35] Public domain.
[36] Trongsa Dzong, Trongsa, Bhutan, public domain.
https://commons.wikimedia.org/wiki/File:Bhutanese_thanka_of_Mt._Meru_and_the_Buddhist_Universe.jpg
[37] Property of the Metropolitan Museum of Art, New York City, public domain.
https://www.metmuseum.org/art/collection/search/60006768#fullscreen